Perspective in Architectural Drawings

Felix König

VNR **VAN NOSTRAND REINHOLD COMPANY**
NEW YORK   CINCINNATI   TORONTO   LONDON   MELBOURNE

Copyright © 1979 by Bauverlag GmbH, Wiesbaden, Berlin
English translation copyright © 1984 by Van Nostrand Reinhold
Library of Congress Catalog Card Number 83-10238

ISBN 0-442-24747-8

Printed in the United States

Published by Van Nostrand Reinhold Company Inc.
135 West 50th Street
New York, New York 10020

Van Nostrand Reinhold Company Limited
Molly Millars Lane
Wokingham, Berkshire RG11 2PY, England

Van Nostrand Reinhold
480 La Trobe Street
Melbourne, Victoria 3000, Australia

Macmillan of Canada
Division of Gage Publishing Limited
164 Commander Boulevard
Agincourt, Ontario M1S 3C7, Canada

16 15 14 13 12 11 10 9 8 7 6 5 4 3 2 1

Library of Congress Cataloging in Publication Data
König, Felix, 1915–
           Perspective in architectural drawings.

   Translation of: Bauwerke in Handzeichungen.
   Includes index.
   1. Perspective.   2. Architectural drawing.   I. Title.
NA2710.K6913   1984   720'.28'4   83-10238
ISBN 0-442-24747-8 (pbk.)

Contents

Foreword

Knowledge and experience are transmitted through the written and spoken word. All the senses are used, including the eye. But form and space are difficult to describe in words, and an immediate impression is gained only when we confront the form or stand within the space.

The image is the best way of conveying an impression to another person. Image was the instrument of painters and graphic artists through the ages.

Then along came photography, which developed into a sophisticated art form. The photographic plate is the medium on which the image is finally fixed. Leonardo da Vinci and Albrecht Dürer were already working with calibrated plates of glass, while von Ranke invented the perspectograph, which was produced by Wolz in Bonn. The image is recorded on a plane, the photographic plate, a technique which has now attained a high degree of perfection.

The task of the draftsman, however, is to visualize the as yet invisible, and so a technique has been developed, the theory of constructive perspective, which borrows much from the realm of photography (in particular, from optics). This technique will become an essential tool for the qualified specialist in producing artistic designs.

This book is thus intended as a genuine guide for the student, and author has made every effort to stick to concepts which recur throughout a wide variety of different exercises. The degree of difficulty and complexity increases from exercise to exercise, but anyone who closely follows the book's line of thought need have no fear of failing to complete the course. Traditional rules and laws are used to guide the student through apparently unfamiliar terrain.

This book is not just for young people who have chosen architecture as their metier, but for everyone who is interested in the subject.

In terms of integration and the search for interprofessional points of reference in general, this is a book that should transcend the rigid compartmentation of schools and colleges.

Finally, the author trusts that today's architects and engineers can use this guide to amplify or refresh forgotten knowledge.

Felix König

1. Introduction to Perspective

The word "perspective" is taken from the Latin and means "viewing through" (*spectare:* to view; *perspectare:* to view through).

Viewing means seeing, observing, perceiving, recognizing, and even assessing or evaluating in relation to known impressions experienced in our environment. The process of learning is the integration of new knowledge. With both our eyes, we see everything simultaneously from two standpoints, and it is this which enables us to see things spatially, (i.e., three-dimensionally) because we can appreciate the size and distance of all objects in relation to one another.

This optical judgment makes everything interdependent, or "optically relative."

People's talents differ and so do their spatial imagination and visual memory. But these skills can be learned, and they are learned primarily through the theory of perspective. Naturally, freehand drawing and plan drawing are preliminary stags in this process.

The theory and practice of perspective require precise learning processes which gradually broaden the mind through the ability to think logically.

Freehand drawing does train our ability to transfer an object directly onto a drawing plane, but is devoid of any knowledge of constructive rules.

This is why the fundamental elements of projection theory and parallelometry (isometry) must first be acquired before proceeding with perspective. As the basis of all project planning, projection theory is dealt with here in a concise manner; more space is given to parallelometry because it plays an essential practical role in the representation of images, even without perspective.

2. Projection Theory

Solids and space have three dimensions: length, width, and height.

Every solid and every space is three-dimensional. Our drawing surface, however, is two-dimensional. Nevertheless, we must give the impression of space, and so a system was invented which governs each dimension and allocates to it a given place within the drawing surface.

The system is based on three faces of a six-sided cube, the bottom and two adjacent sides. The bottom (the ground plan) already lies in the drawing plane.

The other two sides are turned in a vertical plane and "folded" into the drawing plane. The side which is still connected to the ground plan along its edge is always the front elevation, while the side that is not connected to the ground plan but which is turned in toward the front elevation is always the side elevation. Thus, ground plan and front and side elevations are all within the drawing plane (Figures 2.1 and 2.2). For the sake of clarity, we have emphasized the limits of the three faces; the result is a cross—the coordinates—with the reference axes Z-Y and X-Y.

By means of vertical or horizontal projections, i.e., auxiliary lines projected onto the axes, it is possible to determine all the dimensions of a solid or space that we wish to insert into this basic system.

The ground plan tells us about length and width, the front elevation about length and height, and the side elevation about height and width.

The folds between the faces are also called trace lines. The object should not intersect these lines if possible, since this can affect clarity and hamper the thought and learning processes.

If we now insert a solid body into this system, the ground plan, front elevation, and side elevation will offer us a plan view, front view, and side view respectively. The solid is thus projected and analyzed in this way, and becomes a plan from which it is possible to determine all dimensions necessary to model it to a given scale.

Here is an example of scale: Scale 1:100 means 1 cm in the drawing = 1 meter in real life or, as a model, approximately the same size as the plan.

For the purposes of demonstration, it is cheaper to produce a 3-D drawing, while the molded micromodel can help with complex forms.

However, the domain of the architect is the artist's impression.

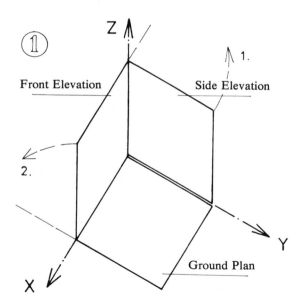

Figure 2.1

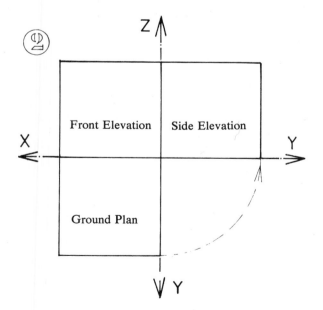

Figure 2.2

3. Parallelometry

Our first task is to illustrate a project based on the projection theory, and once again a system is indispensable. We use the projection theory with its known axes Z-Y and X-Y. We now turn Y to Y to obtain a "tripod" with the axes X, Y, and Z. The tripod is to parallelometry what the co-ordinates are to the projection theory.

Spatial images are created, as shown in Figures 3.1, 3.2, and 3.3, and these are based on the laws of parallelometry. All parallel straight lines of a solid remain parallel in its picture.

The Z-axis should be kept vertical; otherwise, the resulting distortions will deviate from the mind's expectations. There are some inclined images whose effect bears no comparison with the effort that went into making them. It is possible to show certain architectural details in this way, but not larger architectural relationships.

Figure 3.1. The X-axis is determined by angle β; the Y-axis by angle α. The smaller the angles α and β, the "flatter" the picture will appear. Here is a view from above; when the axes run along the front edges of the object, we obtain a view from below (optical illusion). a, b, and h are true sizes (isometry).

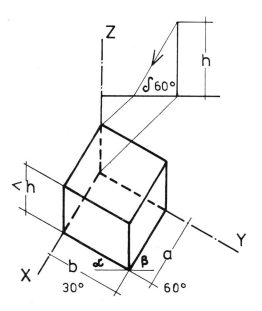

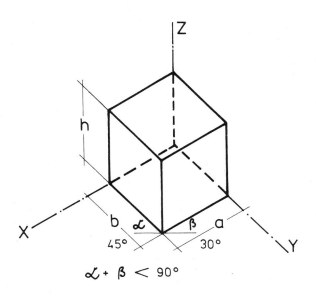

$$\alpha + \beta < 90°$$

Figure 3.2: Cavalier Perspective

The X-axis lies in the trace lines between ground plan and front elevation. The Y-axis is determined by the angle α. γ gives an optical lateral curve to b. The result is a dimetrical image in which 2 sides (a and h) remain true sizes. It is used for architectural details in bird's- and worm's-eye views.

Figure 3.3: Military Perspective

The form of the solid is maintained in ground plan. α and β determine the inclination of the plan to the vertical Z-axis. Generally speaking, these solids are isometric; however when the general angle of vision δ is greater than 45°, h is foreshortened. It is dimetric because 2 sides remain constant. This type of perspective is suitable for smaller objects. Isometric military perspective, however, is suitable for the illustration of large objects in urban planning.

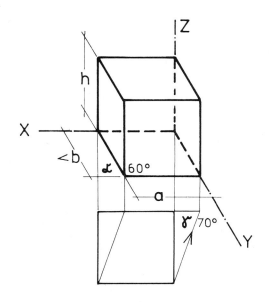

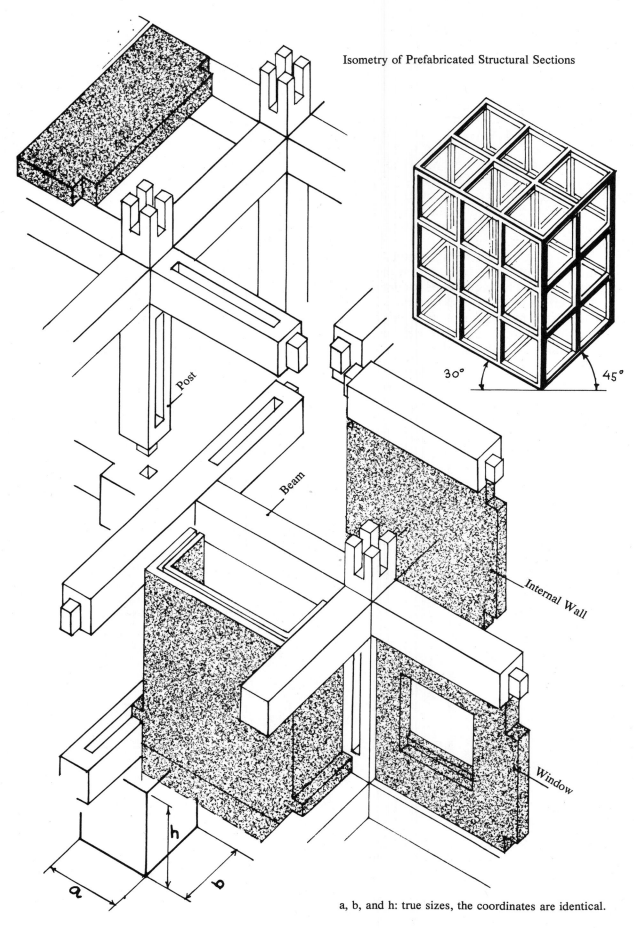

Isometry of Prefabricated Structural Sections

Post

Beam

Internal Wall

Window

30°   45°

h

a

b

a, b, and h: true sizes, the coordinates are identical.

Figure 3.4

Cavalier Perspective as General View (A)

Isometric Structure of a Chest (B)

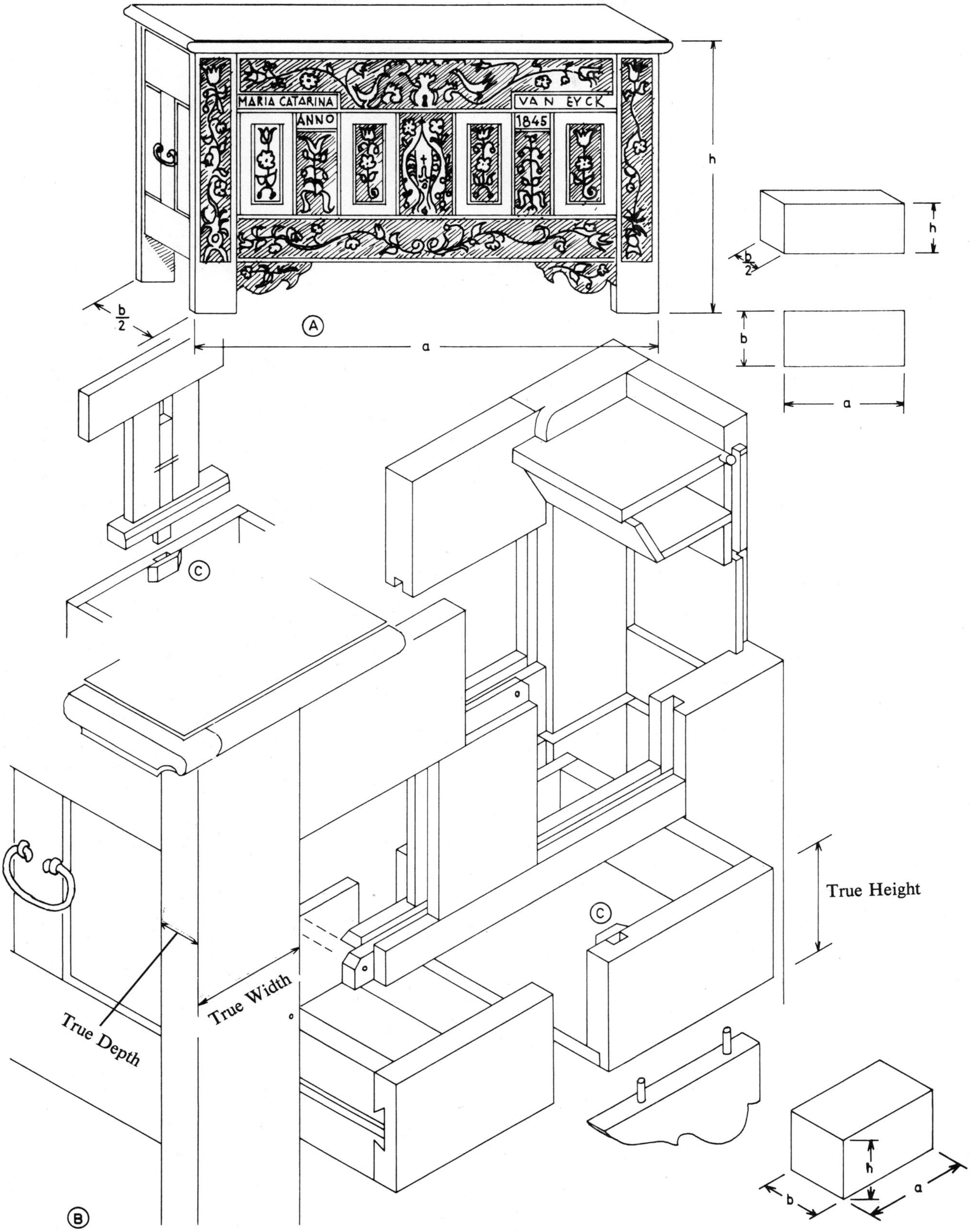

MARIA CATARINA   VAN EYCK

ANNO   1845

h

a

b/2

b/2

b

a

h

(A)

(C)

(C)

True Height

True Width

True Depth

b   h   a

(B)

Lower-Rhenish Chest (from the author's book of the same name)

Figure 3.5

13

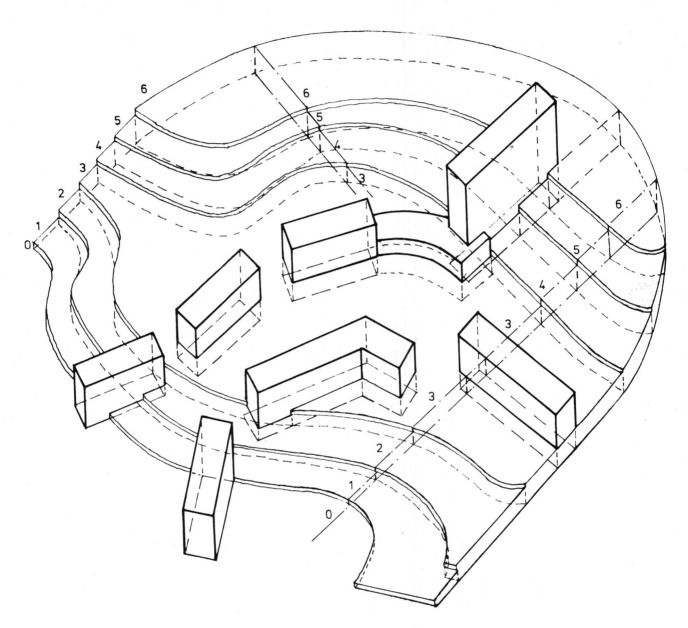

Figure 3.6a

Figure 3.6b

Cavalier Perspective

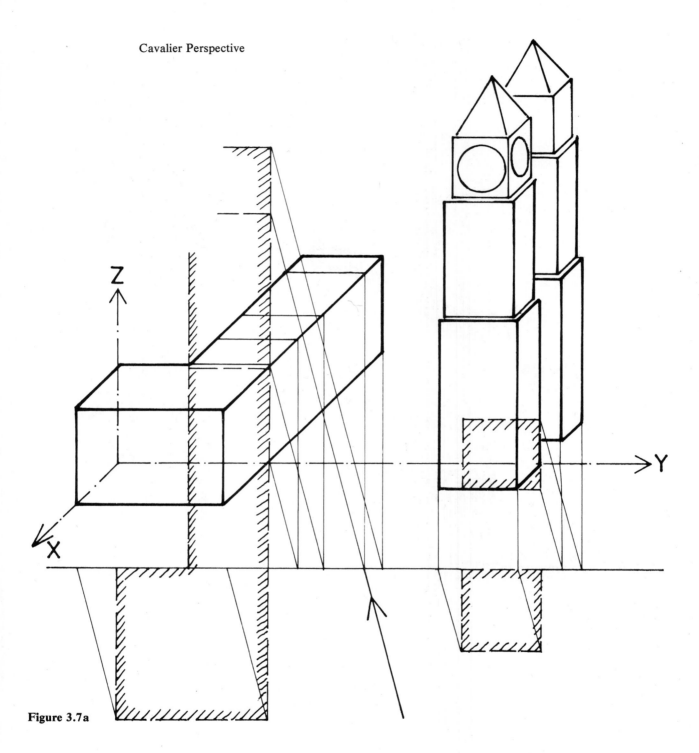

Figure 3.7a

Figure 3.7b

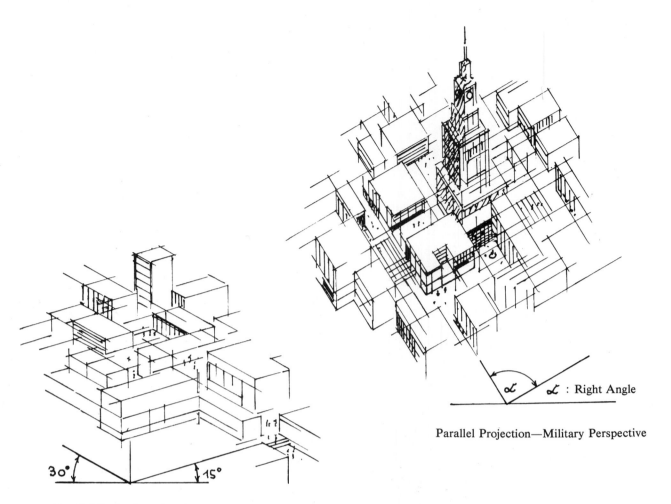

Parallel Projection—Military Perspective

α : Right Angle

Parallel Projection—Isometry

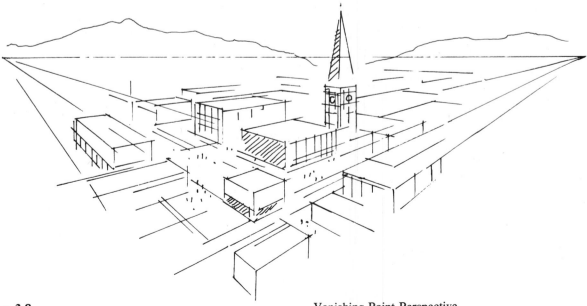

Figure 3.8

Vanishing Point Perspective

4. Regular Relationships

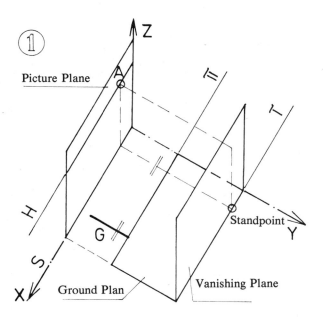

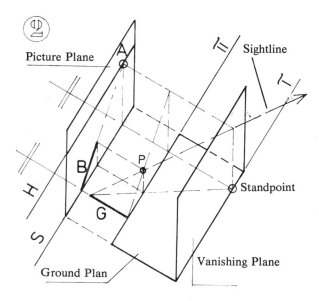

Figure 4.1. The basic concepts of perspective are shown here through parallelometry. Isometric military perspective has been chosen because it retains all right angles in ground plan.

Ground plan and front elevation are shown separately. The vanishing plane in which the observer stands is always parallel to the picture plane π. This chapter is intended to clarify the regular relationships of all components necessary for the construction of a perspective picture. The vanishing line in which the observer stands is always part of the ground plan. The level of the determined in the vanishing plane, as is π, the line on which the picture plane stands. Object G is to be drawn in perspective and is perpendicular to π in this instance.

In front elevation, the picture plane becomes visible as a surface, and this is the drawing surface for all perspective pictures. The chief components of this plane are the trace line S and the horizon H. H always lies on the observer's eye level and should be thought of as a projection of the vanishing plane τ. H is the vanishing line in which all images disappear (vanish) whose objects lie horizontally.

The vanishing point for a horizontal straight line G is determined by the angle at which the line lies to π. The eye pursues this direction as far as π; it also follows it as far as S in the projection in front elevation and from S to the horizon at vanishing point A.

Figure 4.2 shows the construction of the perspective image B from object G.

Since the object starts in π, the image also begins in S. The perspective direction of the image runs toward A. The eye sees the size of the object along a sightline at breakthrough point P in picture plane π. The projection into the front elevation intersects the vanishing line at its end point.

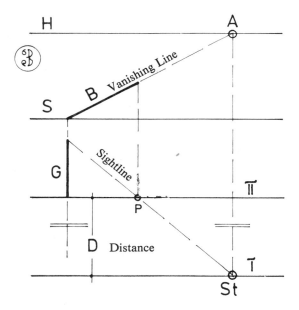

Figure 4.3 is a projection of ground plan and front elevation; all perspectives are constructed in a drawing plane in this way. π and τ are always components of the ground plan, while S and H are always parts of the front elevation. This is a rule that must be strictly observed. Sometimes, ground plan and front elevation overlap for lack of space. Nevertheless, strict adherence to this rule will ensure the success of all perspectives.

5. Some Typical Examples of Perspective

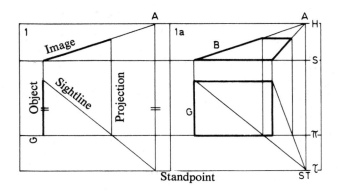

Figure 5.1. Compare Figure 4.3, page 19.

Figure 5.1a is a rectangle whose two sides perpendicular to π are constructed as in Figure 5.1. Sides parallel to the picture plane are also parallel in the picture.

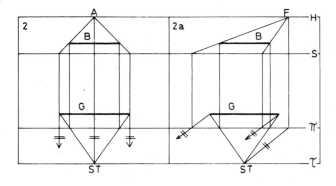

Figures 5.2 and Figure 5.2a. Parallels to π can be constructed with secondary lines which have a common vanishing point.

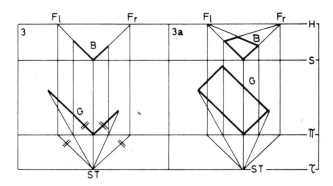

Figure 5.3. Two lines with different directions have two different corresponding vanishing points.

Figure 5.3a. Method for the construction of a rectangle which is inclined to π.

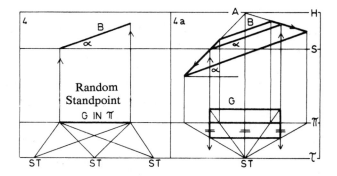

Figure 5.4. A straight line lying in π remains constant irrespective of the observer's standpoint. The angle α is determined in the front elevation.

Figure 5.4a. With a surface which intersects π, the vanishing point of sides perpendicular to π must be determined; only one standpoint must be used.

20

Figure 5.5. A straight line rising at angle α has its vanishing point above the normal horizon vanishing point in H_1 at height $+h$, which is the height of the reference triangle in π. This triangle is turned through 90° into the plan plane.

Figure 5.5a. The same applies to a surface.

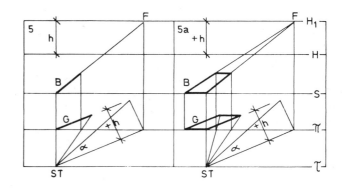

Figure 5.6. An object standing in π never changes (cf. Figure 5.4).

Figure 5.6a. A surface with one side in π has its true height there. It diminishes in size because it lies behind π. If it stood in front of π, it would increase in size.

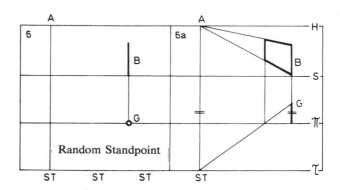

Figure 5.7. A straight line that falls at angle α has its vanishing point beneath the normal horizon vanishing point in H_1 at height $-h$, which is the height of the reference triangle in π.

Figure 5.7a. The same applies to a surface.

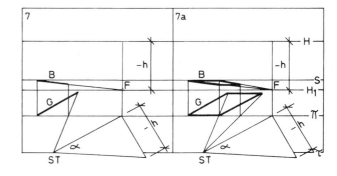

Figures 5.8 and 5.8a. The same applies here as in Figures 5.5 and 5.5a.

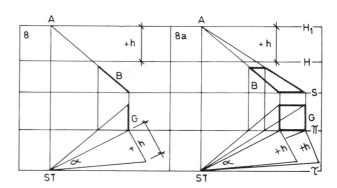

6. Component Points

Figure 6.1 shows the breakthrough process in Figure 4.3 on page 19 for comparison.

Figure 6.2. If we now turn object and standpoint about their axes in π and project the resulting points onto S and H, then the connection between the trace point and the component point in H is the first geometric location for the end point of the picture. The second geometric location is the vanishing line at A.

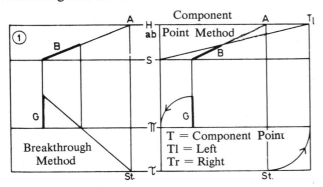

Figure 6.3. Each straight line is turned in π. The component point which belongs to the left line of the object appears to the right on the horizon, while the component point for the right-hand line lies to the left.

Figure 6.4. A straight line has only one component point.

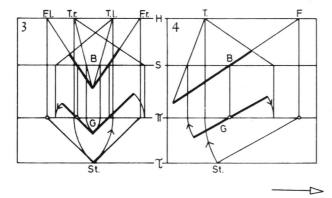

Figure 6.7. For long facades, we can use the breakthrough process to create staggered sections, but the component point method achieves the desired effect more quickly and accurately. In this illustration, the ground plan is still turned in π. We can immediately place the facade in S and join up the facade sections with the component point.

The vanishing line of the facade is then divided in perspective; it can also be divided in height (floors).

Figure 6.5. Two turns have two component points.

Figure 6.6. Turning must always be done in π. The straight lines in π must be brought to the trace line.

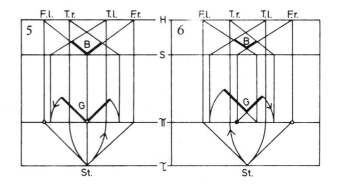

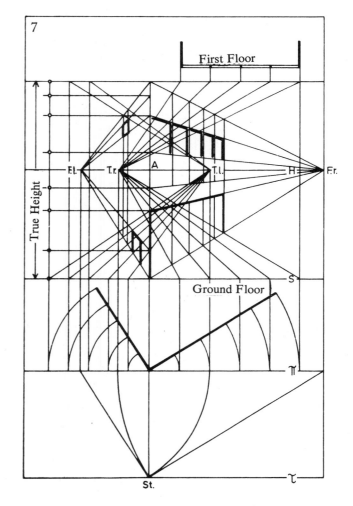

7. Distance Points

Imagine a vanishing point circle seen in front elevation (Figure 7). The vanishing points themselves are determined by the sides of pyramids in plan view, which are in turn determined by the four directions of the diagonals. Eyepoint A is governed by all sides that are perpendicular to π. Since the distances from A to Dl, Do, Dr, and Du in front elevation equal the distance D in ground plan from St to π, this system is called the "Distance Point Method."

The construction of the two cubes to form their perspective images is governed by their specific position in ground plan and their specific height (S) in front elevation.

The left-hand cube is smaller than lifesize because it lies behind π. The right-hand cube has its true size in the surface that lies in π. It then increases in size because the solid itself lies in front of π. The vanishing points on the circle have the same function as in the component point technique (Figures 6.2 to 6.7).

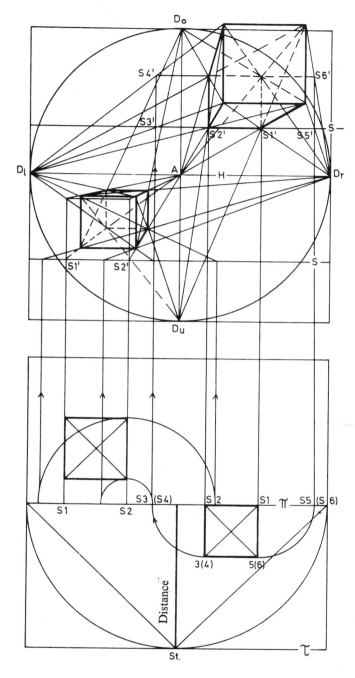

8. Perspectives with Three Sides

In ground plan and side elevation, parallel lines and surfaces are determined by diagonals (three-sided projection).

The ground plan indicates the position of the objects. With side elevation, therefore, we just need the heights of all the objects in order to show the images in front elevation. As with the ground plan, the breakthrough process is used here as proof of this statement. A number of trace lines (S) indicate true heights and widths.

The illustration below is offered as a study object for meditation. The student will realize that any position of an object can be shown in perspective—objects behind π diminish in size, those in front of π get larger. A is the central vanishing point for all straight lines that lie perpendicular to π. Dl, Do, Dr, and Du are the vanishing points of all diagonals (cf. Distance Point Method, page 23.)

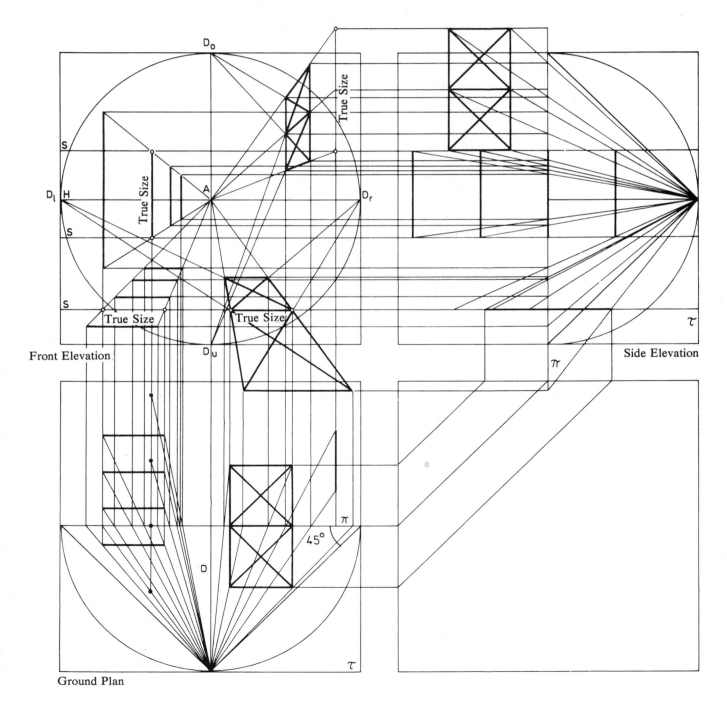

9. Unattainable Vanishing Points

Figure 9.1: Construction Using Trace Point/ Vanishing Point Method

Here the left-hand vanishing point is unattainable. The line 1,2 is brought to the trace in π and projected to S in front elevation. S also contains the true height, which can be inserted here. The first geometric location is obtained by joining the trace points with the vanishing point on the right (Fl r). We use the breakthrough process to obtain the second geometric location and hence points 1′, 2′, 3′, 4′. The remaining construction is easily seen.

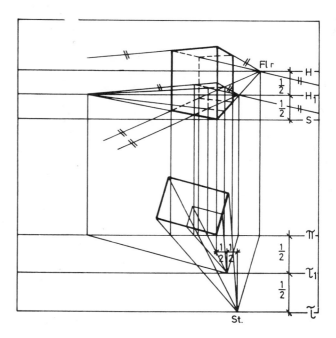

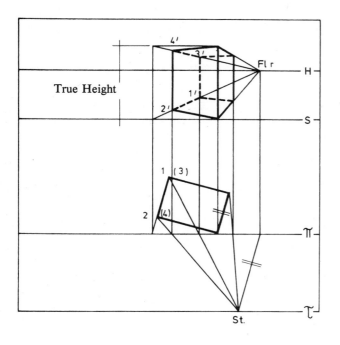

Figure 9.2 can be produced by reducing the scale to one-eighth and retaining form and attitude. All dimensions must be halved: length, width, and height of the solid, distance, and horizon. The image of the small solid is obtained with the normal trace point/vanishing point method. We use the breakthrough method to obtain the first geometric locations for the vertical sides of the large image. Since both solids are in the same plane, their front sides are flush. All the rear and upper sides of the larger solid are obtained by the parallel displacement of all the relevant sides of the smaller solid.

Figure 9.3: Construction with Vanishing Scales

In H of the front elevation, we can draw a trapezium whose left edge runs parallel to D. D is divided into, say, six equal parts, likewise the left edge of the trapezium.

The connection and extension of these numbered divisions would end in an unattainable vanishing point. Below H, all perspective lines of the object can be interpolated within this system; the same system can be used above H as well.

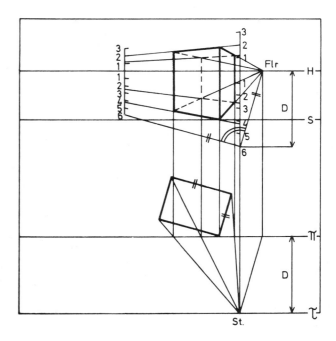

10. Perspective Division

Figure 10.1. The surface of an image can be perspectively divided if we relate vanishing point and standpoint to a straight line divided equally to our own choice. The breakthrough points in π give the projection points for the perspective division.

When the object is behind π, it diminishes in size.

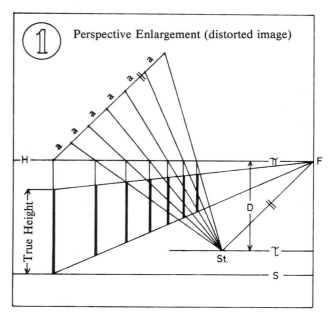

Figure 10.2. Here the object lies in front of π. The resulting enlargement can cause distortion if the angle of vision is too great.

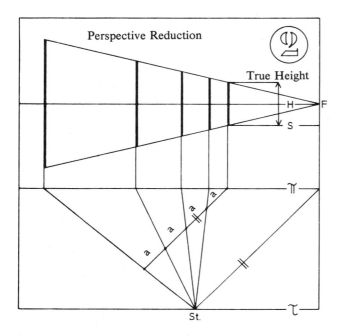

Figure 10.3. Perspective division can also be done with a point P placed at random on H. The rhythm must keep to the scale set by the intersecting line.

If the division gets too close to the edge of the picture, a fresh division can be done upward, with its own scale and rhythm.

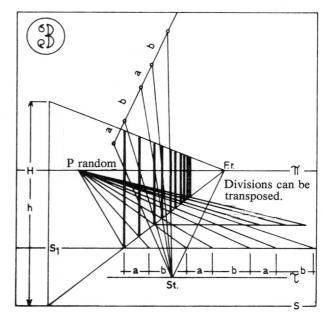

11. Practical Examples

Figure 11.1: Street Scene

This street scene is in dual vanishing point perspective. π is determined by two building corners. The true height of the building is in the intersecting points. All major parts of buildings were projected in front elevation using the breakthrough method, while all true heights were measured from S. The attitude of the buildings determines the vanishing points that lie at the left- and right-hand edges of the picture on the horizon. The result is simple cubic solids. Partitioning is related to the window lines, which are also found and projected in π with the breakthrough method. Heights are plotted where the picture plane touches the object. The true width in S is where roads cut through π. Points of intersection are connected to the vanishing points. Quadrants at the road junction would be elliptical in the picture—they are not shown here because they are not very conspicuous. Now comes the illustrator's routine work: illustrating a scene with a few telling points. The perspective locations of the trees are also taken from the ground plan. Their approximate heights can be found by the trace point method (see ground plan left).

The vanishing points for the shop window blinds are determined by the angles of inclination α and β (cf. guide triangles in ground plan and height indications hα and hβ, which are measured off on H and which give the vanishing points for the blinds above the horizon vanishing points). The reach of the blinds is shown in the ground plan.

An otherwise somber construction has been provided with some attractive illustration here, because the artistic accent is meant to be a feature of this book.

Figure 11.2: Half-Timbered House at the Edge of a Forest

π lies in the rear gable wall at a relatively long distance from τ, while H is low down. The first geometric locations in π are determined by the breakthrough method. The eaves are constructed through vanishing point A and the true heights in S. Roof pitches are kept true to life because their angles are parallel to π!

The road gradient starts in π—the gradient angle is α. h is obtained with the guide triangle to π with α. The road's vanishing point lies at a distance h above A (F. Str). Details are drawn in freehand.

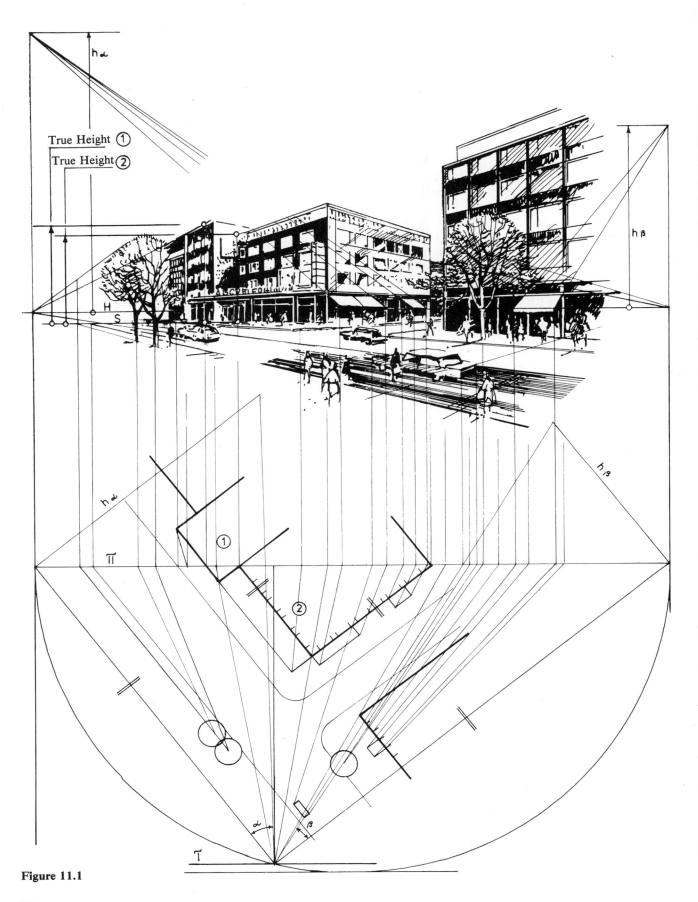

True Height ①
True Height ②

H
S

hα
hβ

①
②

π

α β

T

Figure 11.1

28

Figure 11.2

F.Str = vanishing point of road
T.h. = height to eaves

29

Figure 11.3: Conservatory

The form of the conservatory with all its angles gives us three vanishing points. True height is in the corner of the house. Height to eaves and roof pitch are marked in front elevation. The house walls can now be constructed in perspective. Perspective roof pitch starts at the gable with the two vanishing points which are given by $+h$ and $-h$. These are found with α in τ, the dip lines of the roofs (rafters) above and below F_1, and the resulting guide triangle. Pool edges, door, and palm trees are accurately positioned, while windowpanes and rafter spacing have been freely selected to perspective, and likewise the remaining detail.

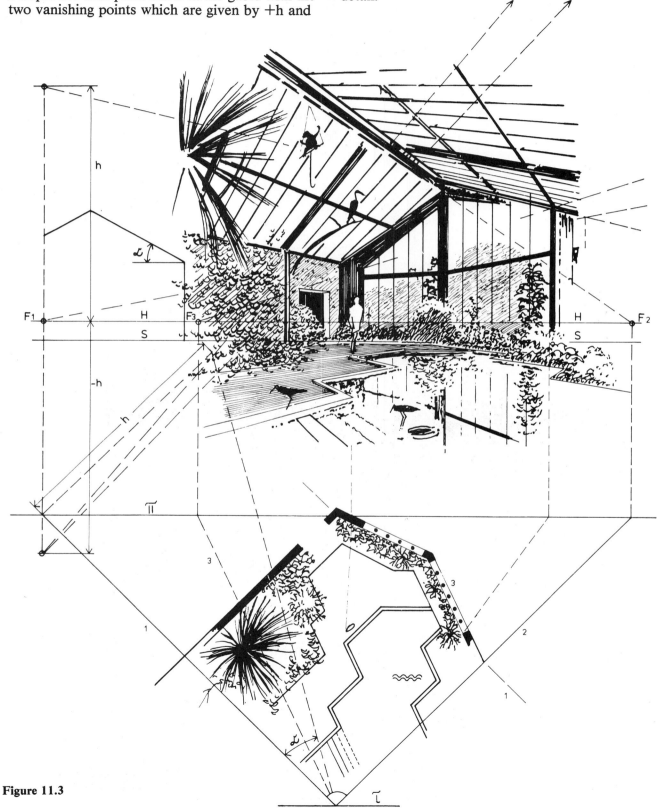

Figure 11.3

30

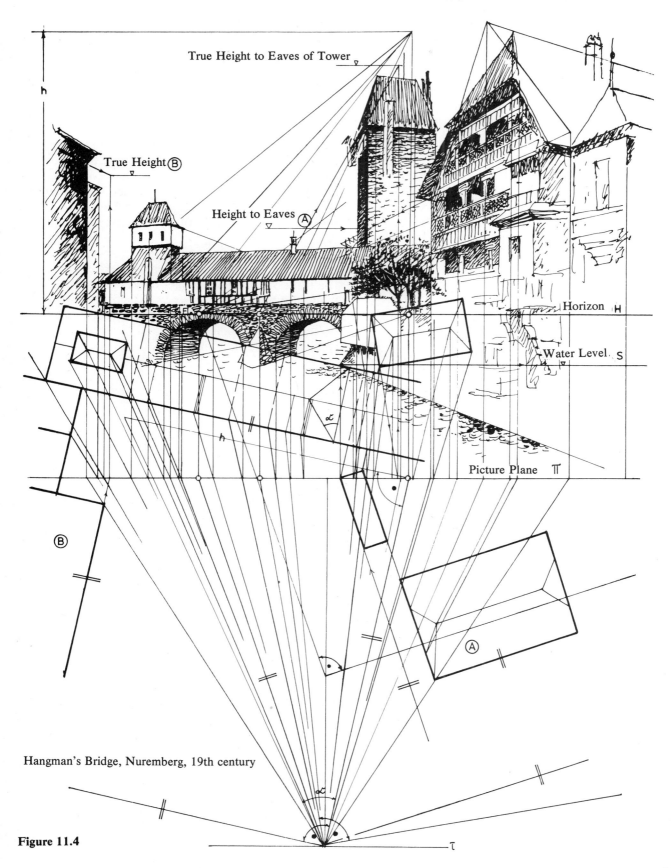

True Height to Eaves of Tower

True Height $\textcircled{B}$

Height to Eaves $\textcircled{A}$

Horizon H

Water Level S

Picture Plane π

$\textcircled{B}$

$\textcircled{A}$

Hangman's Bridge, Nuremberg, 19th century

Figure 11.4

Figure 11.4: Nuremberg—Hangman's Bridge

All the essential constructive details are shown in the drawing. It is important here to study all visible structures in the light of known rules and verify them against knowledge obtained from this book so far. A few hints will prove clearer than a complex explanation:

1. All essential structures are marked in bold line on the plan view.
2. The bridge is practically parallel and so hardly vanishes; it tapers to the left by the width of a stroke.
3. Fl is the vanishing point for building A.
   Fr is the vanishing point for building B.
4. The true eave height for building A in front elevation is given by the trace of the gable in ground plan to π.

   The true eave height for building B in front elevation is given by the trace of the eave in ground plan to π.

   The eave height of the tower is also constructed as with A and B.

   Ridge heights have been freely assumed but would be easy to determine by the same principle.
5. With α in ground plan (pitch of bridge roof), we obtain h and hence the vanishing point for the dip lines of the pantiles. All other details have been shown according to old illustrations.

Figure 11.5: Nuremberg—the Castle

The picture plane π is behind the site plan. In this way, it is possible to create a larger, clearer picture from a relatively small plan.

Certain vanishing points lie on a drawing plane which was subsequently cut away; thus the eaves vanish in a credible manner. The first geometric locations of the buildings are determined using the breakthrough method. The traces of the large central gable end can be seen in the front elevation. The connection with A and the associated projections give us the first geometric locations from the breakthrough method. We thus obtain the enlarged image of the gable wall. Building 1 (see ground plan) is found by the same principle.

The elevation of the rectangular tower is marked on the right. The breakthrough method is used to obtain the initial geometric locations, while the picture of the tower is achieved with the trace point method, with the aid of the true sizes. Other details are taken from old illustrations or freely drawn by the author.

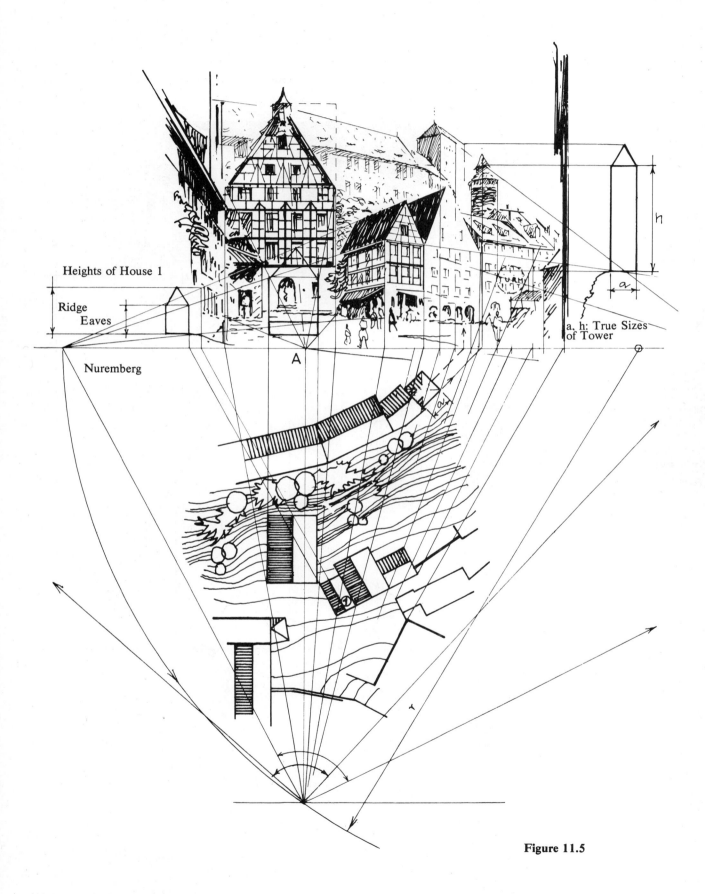

Heights of House 1

Ridge

Eaves

Nuremberg

A

a, h: True Sizes of Tower

h

a

Figure 11.5

Figures 11.6.1.–11.6.6. Examples of rapid sketching of constructive and architectural situations.

Simple application of the trace point and breakthrough methods.

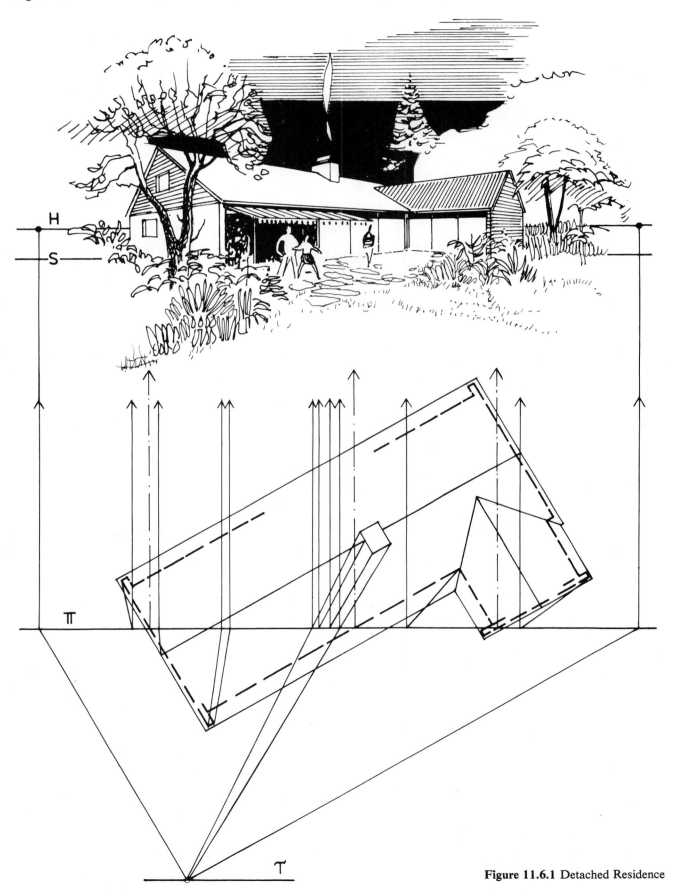

Figure 11.6.1 Detached Residence

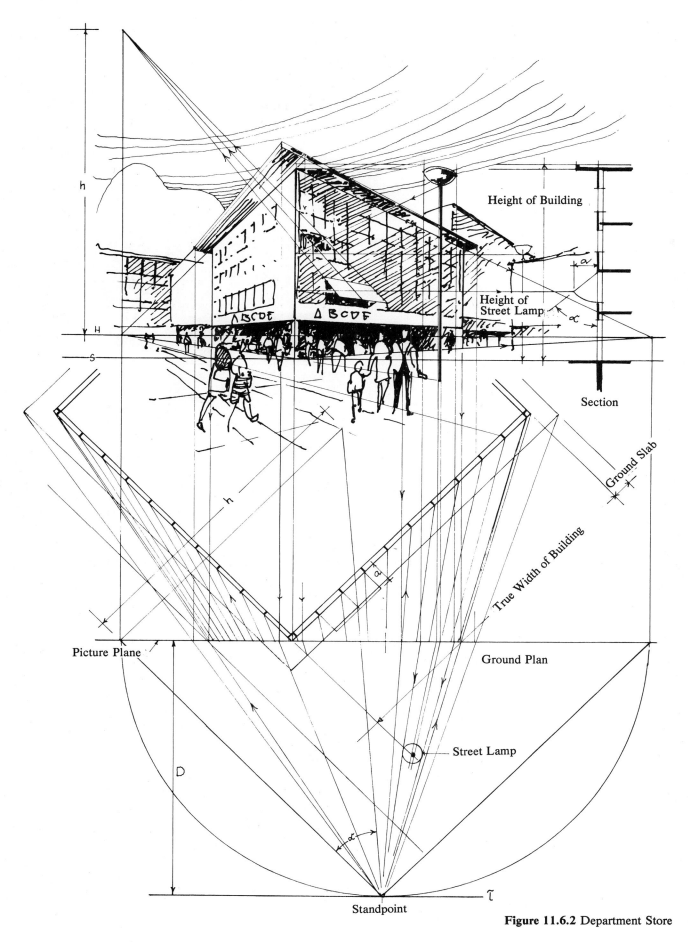

h

H

S

Height of Building

Height of
Street Lamp

α

α

Section

h

a

True Width of Building

Ground Slab

Picture Plane

Ground Plan

Street Lamp

D

α

l

Standpoint

Figure 11.6.2 Department Store

35

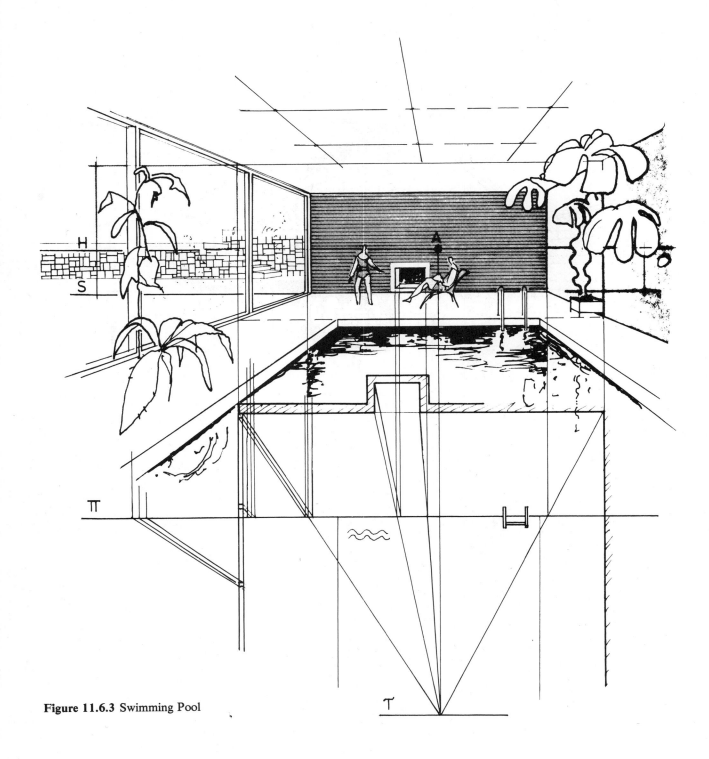

Figure 11.6.3 Swimming Pool

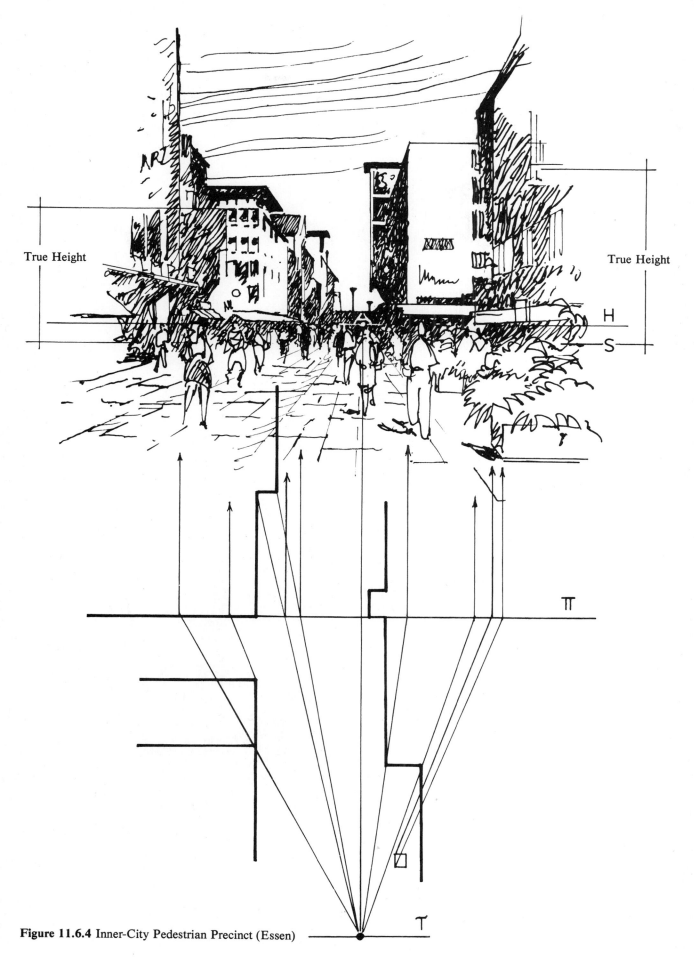

True Height

True Height

H

S

Π

T

Figure 11.6.4 Inner-City Pedestrian Precinct (Essen)

37

Figure 11.6.5 Octagonal Tower Dwelling and Village Green

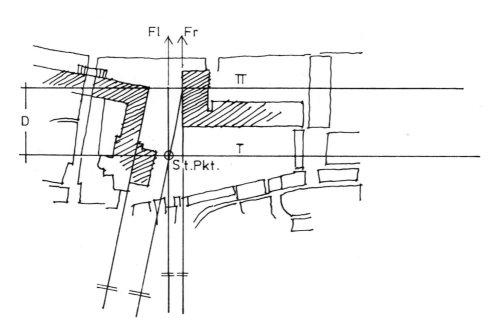

Figure 11.6.6 Venice

Figure 11.7: Atrium—Interior Courtyard

Construction with unattainable vanishing point (Fl) by means of breakthrough and trace point methods (cf. Figure 9.1). Since ground plan and picture coincide (this is a frequent occurrence in practice owing to lack of space), clarity is forfeited, which is why our freehand drawing has been shown separately.

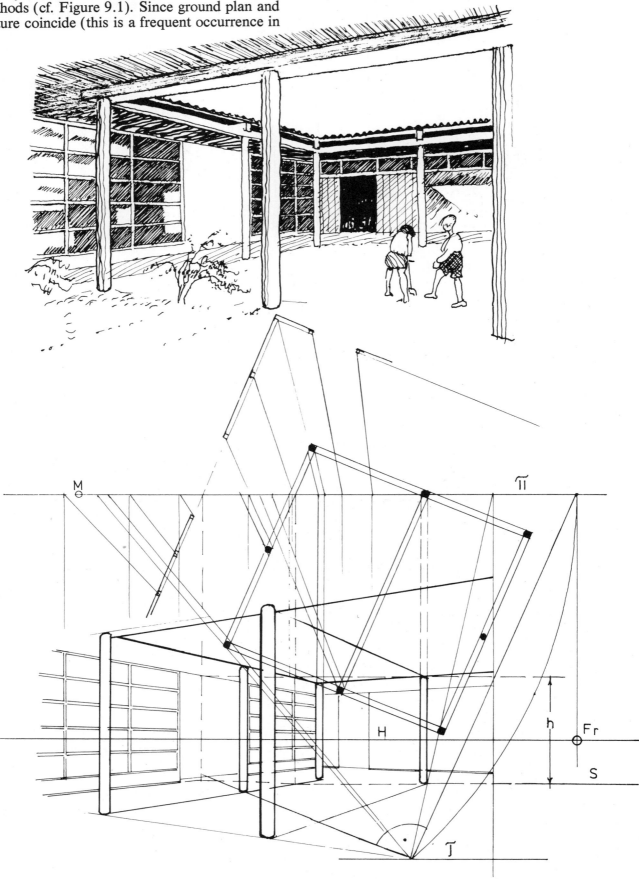

Figure 11.8: High-Rise Building with Unattainable Vanishing Point

The drawing clearly shows how to construct a perspective when the vanishing point is un-attainable.

The dotted lines are the plan view. Horizon (H) and picture plane (π) coincide here (to save space).

Vanishing point Fl is attainable and determined by the position of the buildings. A right angle is formed at the standpoint, resulting in a free arm (-5, -5) which runs parallel to the side of the building but which cannot attain vanishing point Fr. We now draw a line parallel to Distance D and as close as possible to the right-hand edge of the paper, obtaining a trapezium with that part of the horizon.

D is now divided into 5, as is the line drawn parallel to D at paper's edge. The connecting lines would all lead to vanishing point Fr.

The same is done above the horizon. We are now able to interpolate all building corners into this perspective grid—i.e., all corners which should lead to the unattainable vanishing point.

All other constructive details are shown in the diagram. The illustration is shown separately.

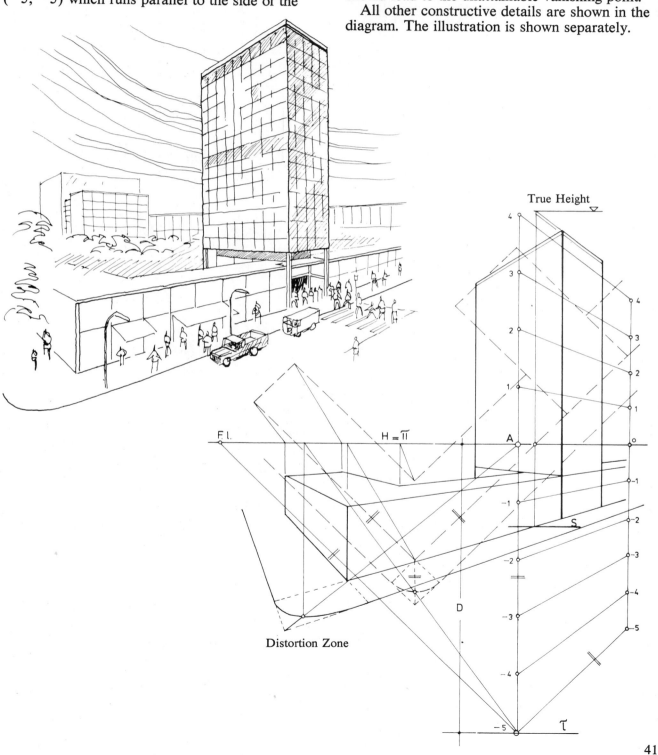

True Height

F.l.   H = $\overline{\Pi}$

Distortion Zone

41

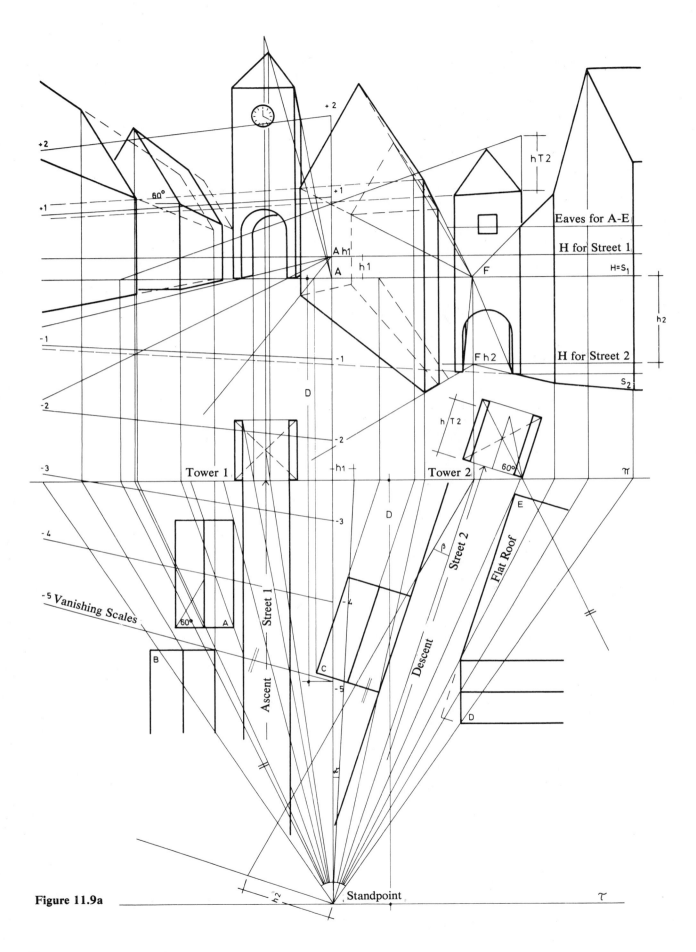

Figure 11.9a

42

Figure 11.9b

Figure 11.9a: Rothenburg on Tauber (Plönlein)—an Unattainable Vanishing Point

This construction is based on a thorough understanding of all knowledge and skills so far acquired. The scene includes five buildings, two towers, and one rising and one falling street.

The front wall of tower 1 lies in S_1, which is also the true height of the eaves. A is the vanishing point for this tower. Since the front arch lies in π as a semicircle, the parallel rear arch is also a semicircle.

Since S_1 is also in the horizon, street level 0 is at the foot of the archway. Vanishing point Ah_1 for the rising street 1 is determined by h_1, which is in turn found with D, α, and π by means of the so-called guide triangle.

The street vanishes through the archway to vanishing point Ah_1 and widens as it falls toward the observer. The street rises higher up behind the tower.

Buildings A and B are also central perspectives with eyepoint at A. The roof pitch of 60° is retained in the picture because the gables are parallel to π. The bases of the buildings fall with the street.

We obtain F from the attitude of buildings C, E, and tower 2. The falling street to tower 2 ends at 0 in S_2. Vanishing point Fh_2 lies beneath F at a distance of h_2. The street vanishes through the arch of T_2 (tower 2) to F_2 and widens out as it rises back up to the observer. In the tower and behind the tower, the street runs horizontal to F. Building D has the eyepoint A. Roof ridge and eaves run horizontal because they are parallel to π. Only vanishing point F can be used for building C and tower 2; the second vanishing point Fl is unattainable. Some assistance here is provided by the perspective grid of the vanishing scales. D is shifted into H. The trapezium with the divisions on D and the left-hand parallel—with the same projected up above the horizon—provides the perspective attitudes toward the unattainable vanishing point for building C and tower 2.

Figure 11.9b: Illustration from Plönlein, Drawn Freehand

43

12. The Circle in Perspective Principles

All circles parallel to π remain circles. They enlarge or diminish according to whether they lie in front of or behind π. All other positions of a circle give ellipses, provided the circle lies in front of τ.

Circles which are tangent to τ give parabolas. Circles which intersect τ give hyperbolas.

12.1 Ellipses

Figure 12.1.1 shows the construction of a circle with the aid of a square we obtain from the sides perpendicular to π.

The trace point and breakthrough method gives us the perspective image of the square.

All points on the circle which are enclosed within the square are incorporated in the image of the square. The result is an ellipse.

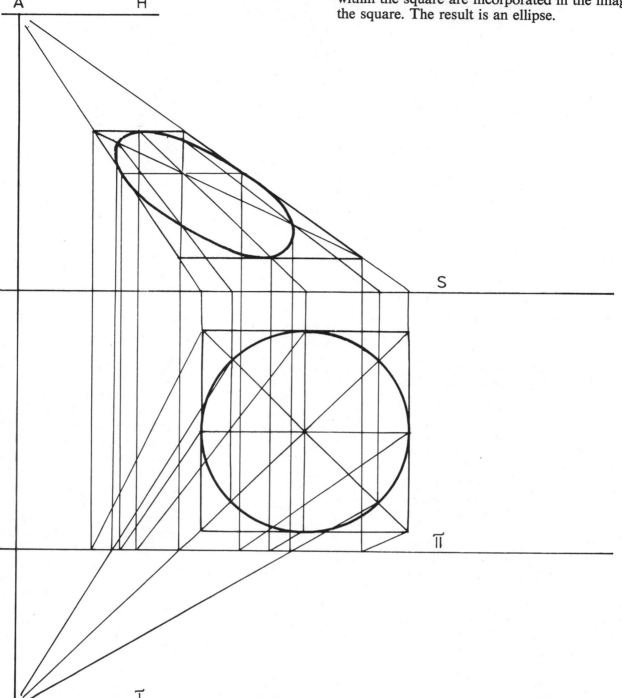

Figure 12.1.2. The circle is enclosed within a trapezium. We take a distance point D to the vanishing point. All secondary lines for trapezium and circle are drawn at 45°. The trace point method gives the first geometric locations through the perspective lines to D.

The traces of the oblique trapezium sides both lead to their vanishing points (a special case) and together with the main sightline provide the second geometric locations in the emerging perspective image. The result is an ellipse enclosed in a rectangle. M is the perspective center of the ellipse. Tangent points 1 and 3 intersect the main sightline at point 5.

All lines which pass through point 5↑ in the ellipse are halved.

(Conjugated diameters), e.g., 3'-5' = 5'-1' or 2'-5' = 5'-4' (ecliptic).

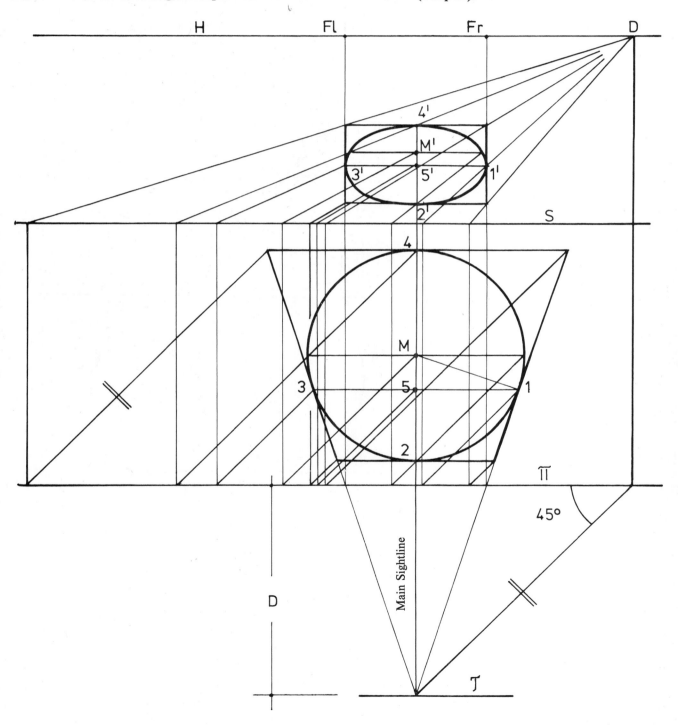

Figure 12.1.3a: Cylinder

Circular construction with the aid of a trapezium
(cf. Figure 12.1.2).

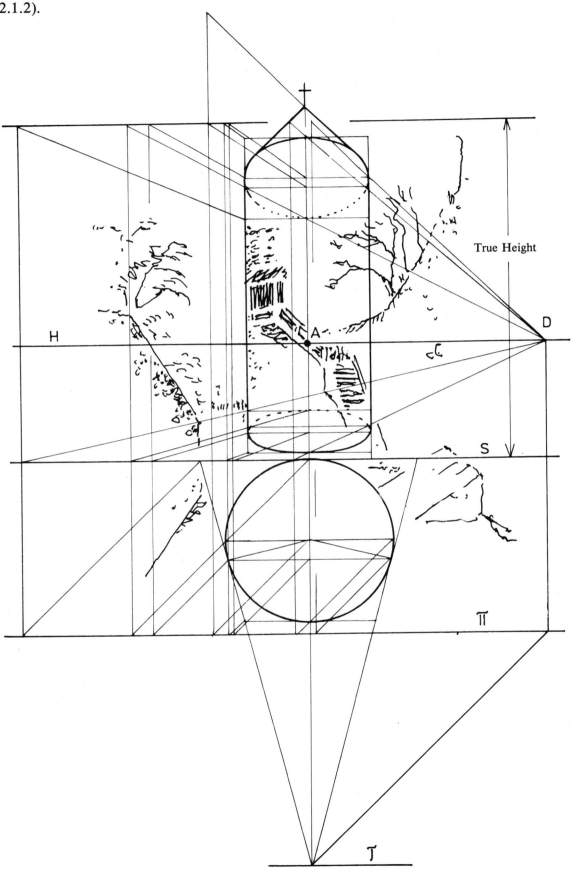

Figure 12.1.3b (cf. Figure 12.1.3a). Freehand
drawing of prison tower, Rothenburg o.T.

Figure 12.1.4. Construction using A and eight auxiliary points on the circle, with trace point and breakthrough method. The perspective image is an ellipse with perspective center.

The outer lines are not tangents, since they intersect the circle very slightly!

Figure 12.1.5 shows the construction of a vertical semicircle.

From the basic attitude, we obtain A in H. The true height lies in the intersecting point of π with the baseline of the semicircle. It must be projected in front elevation.

Using the breakthrough method, we obtain the projection points for the auxiliary lines of the rotated semicircle. These are projected into front elevation and provide the first geometric locations for the semiellipse. Heights h_1, h_2, and h_3 are now joined to A to give the second geometric locations. The points of intersection are connected in similar fashion. The result is a semiellipse.

The bridge, with its detail and reflection forming the full ellipse, is drawn freehand.

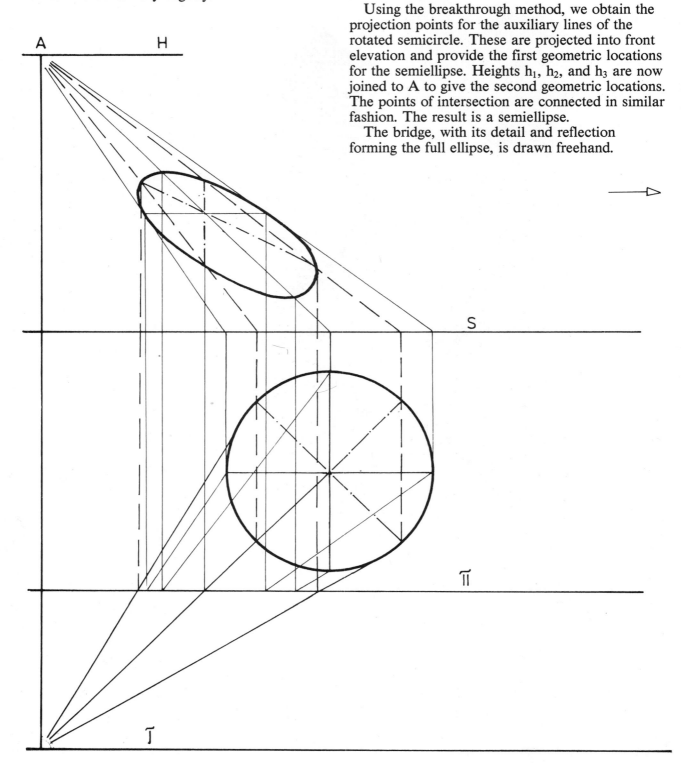

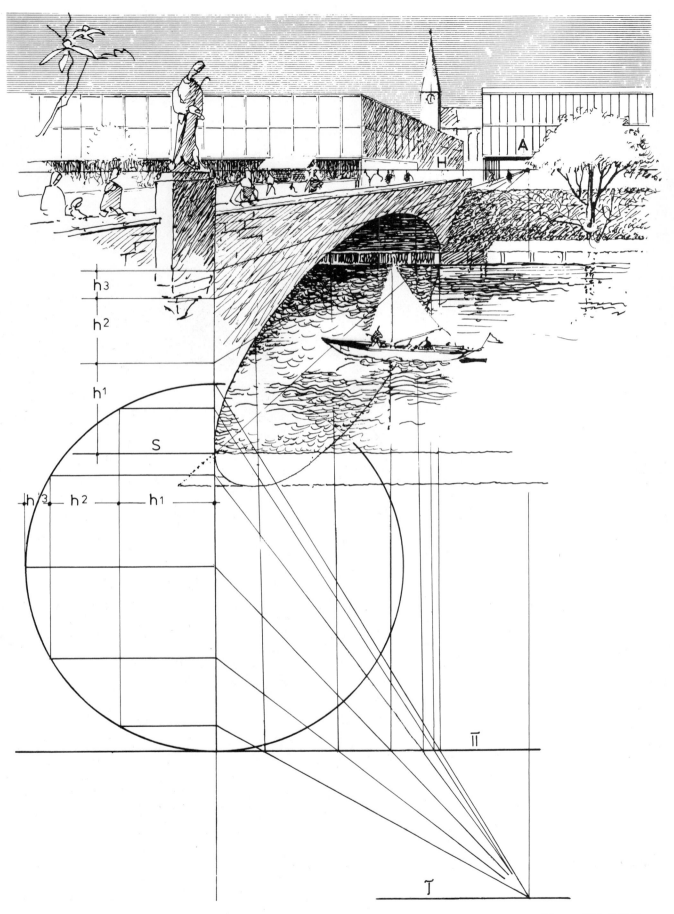

Figure 12.1.5 Bridge

49

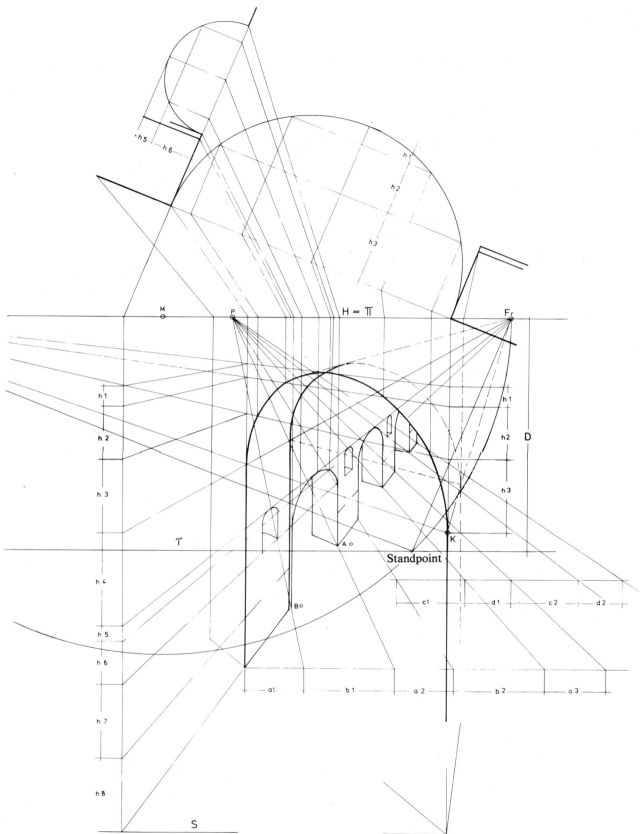

Figure 12.1.6a

50

Figure 12.1.6b

Figure 12.1.6a: Arch Between Nave and Dome of St. Peter's, Rome

The horizon H and picture plane π coincide. With the given position of the ground plan and standpoint, the right-hand vanishing point is visible, while the left-hand vanishing point (Fl) was used on a larger plan. Vanishing scales could have been used here in place of the unattainable vanishing point, but would have sacrificed clarity.

The true size of the main arch has its right-hand corner in π, while the left-hand corner of the arch is traced to π. This is also the location for true sizes.

The auxiliary points above the rotated semi-circle have the heights h_1, h_2, and h_3.

Their projections are drawn to π by the breakthrough method and projected into the picture as the first geometric locations.

The impost height K is determined on the projection of the right-hand pillar. It is selected such that the arch does not intersect H or π. Heights h_1, h_2, and h_3 are now plotted and taken to Fl. They form the second geometric locations whose points of intersection linked to the first geometric locations give a semiellipse.

The arch facing the nave is constructed in the same way, allowing for perspective foreshortening. To the left of the picture, the true heights have been plotted once more and can be used to ascertain the perspective image of the pillar. As we can see, this pillar is greatly foreshortened.

The first arch of the nave is also constructed using trace point and breakthrough methods. Arch heights h_5 and h_6 are plotted in the projection of the trace point, as are the true pillar heights. The subsequent arches and pillars are unattainable by means of the breakthrough method, and so we must resort to the law of perspective division (Figure 10.3).

Points Bo and Ao are known.

From a random point P in H, we draw lines through Bo and Ao on a random basis. The rhythm which we find on that basis must be continued by analogy to the position of the arch; for example: short, long, short, long . . . in this instance, a_1, b_1, a_2, b_2, a_3, and so on. In this way, we obtain the base points for all the visible arches. The heights are already known.

If this sequence becomes too long on the plan, however, the same method can be used a little higher up on the plan. The rhythm stays the same, but the dimensions are smaller (cf. perspective divisions, Figure 10.3).

Figure 12.1.6b. The illustration is drawn freely after the character and style of Italian High Renaissance around the framework provided by the construction (Figure 12.1.6a).

12.2 Parabolas

Figure 12.2. A horizontal circle touches τ. π and S coincide. One diameter of the circle stands perpendicular to π as a main axis and determines the vanishing point A on H. The true size of the circle lies in π/S, and the main axis of the parabola runs through point 5 to A. The other points 1 to 7 marked at random on the main axis are projected by the breakthrough method from π onto the perspective axis, where they are identified as 1m to 7m. On the main axis of the circle,

secants are plotted through points 2 to 7 and the resulting points on the circle are projected onto π. These trace points vanish to A. In this way, they constitute second geometric locations which intersect the first geometric locations, which consist of the horizontal lines running through 2 to 7. We thus obtain 2 to 7 l on the left and 2 to 7 r on the right. With all points connected in the appropriate manner, the result is a parabola.

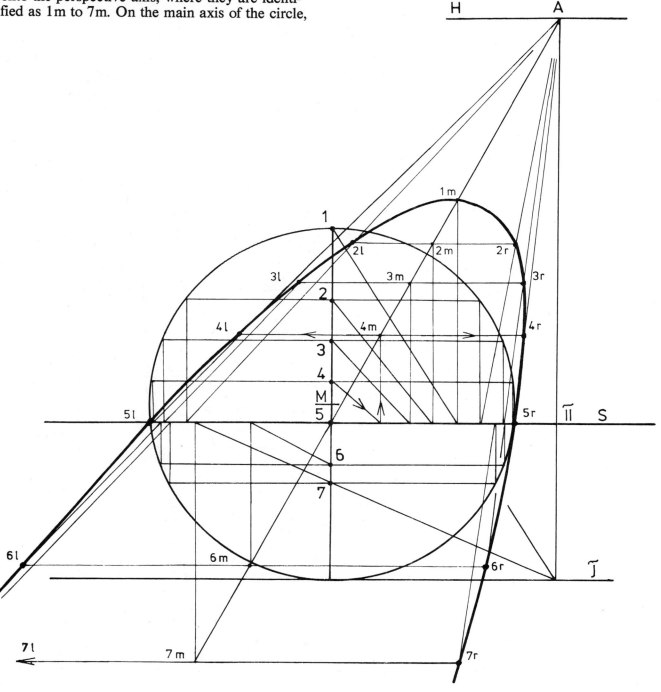

12.3 Hyperbolas

Figure 12.3.1. A horizontal circle is intersected by τ. π and S coincide. One diameter of the circle lies perpendicular to π as the main axis and determines the vanishing point A on H. The true size of the circle lies in π. The main perspective axis runs through point 3 to A. The other points 1 to 5 marked at random on the main axis are projected from π onto the perspective axis by means of the breakthrough method, and are called 1m to 5m.

Secants are plotted on the main axis through points 2 to 5, and the resulting points on the circle are projected onto π. These trace points vanish to A. In this way, they constitute second geometric locations, which intersect with the first geometric locations that consist of the horizontal lines that run through 2m to 5m. Thus we find 2 to 4 l on the left (5 l is unattainable) and 2 to 5 r on the right.

When all points are connected in the appropriate manner, we obtain a hyperbola.

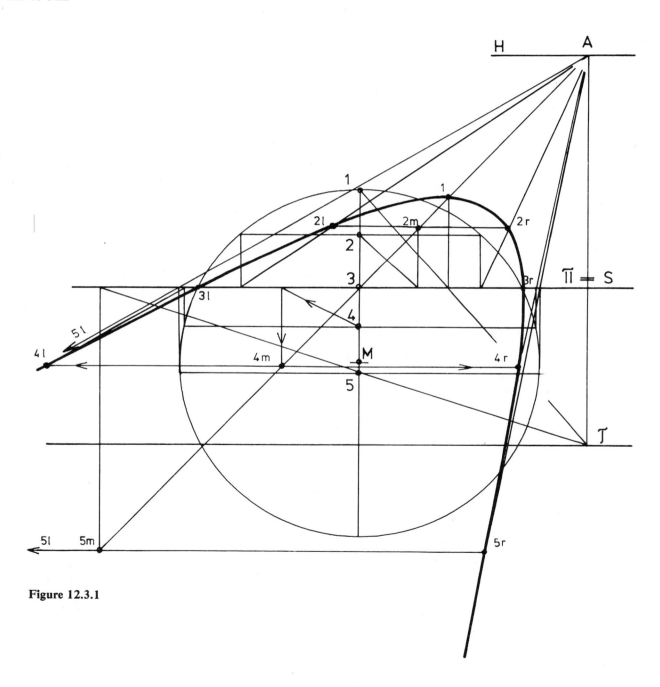

Figure 12.3.1

Figure 12.3.2. A round pool as an urban feature appears as a hyperbola; see Figure 12.3.1.

The sides of the square are constructed as central perspective and shown only in sketch form.

Figure 12.3.3. The freely drawn curve of a beach is constructed with three auxiliary points by the trace point and breakthrough methods; likewise, the apartments. The palm lends the picture an exotic flavor.

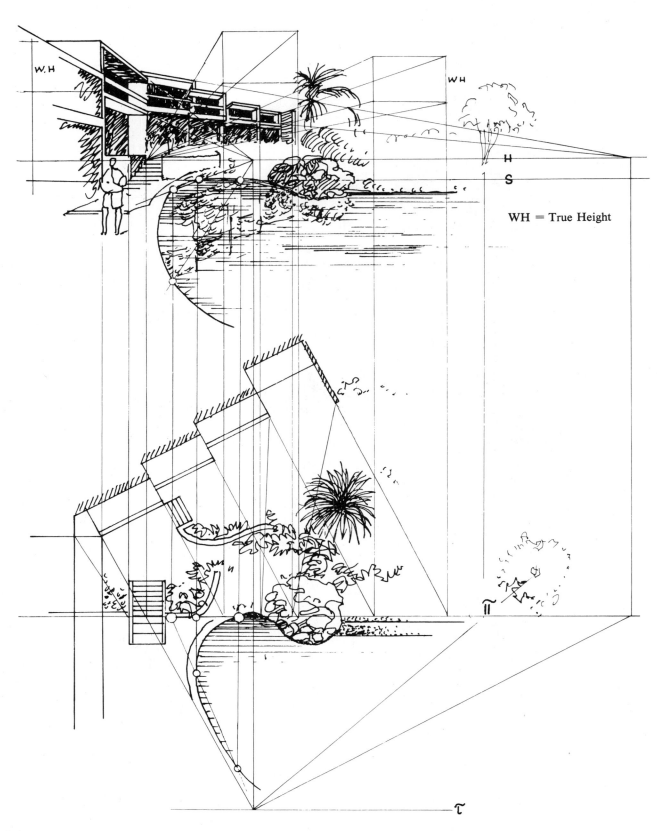

WH = True Height

13. Shadow Cast from a Remote Light Source

Shadows are caused by a light source and an object standing on a horizontal ground plane. The light source in this case is the sun, which is at a remote distance and whose rays may therefore be taken to be parallel. Like all other parallels in perspective, the sun's light rays vanish and so have a vanishing point.

The vanishing point L^o is governed by the solar angle α, the angle of incidence β, and the standpoint of the observer. β becomes visible in the triangle in which h indicates the height of the solar vanishing point above H. Of course, the sun casts shadows whether there is an observer present or not, but the perspective form of the shadows depends upon the observer's standpoint.

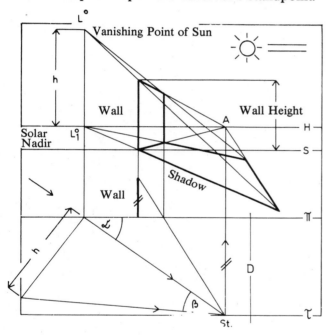

Figure 13.1. The observer sees the sun at vanishing point L^o (L from lux = light). It is as it were the breakthrough point on the picture in front elevation. When the observer can see the sun, we speak of counterlight. When the sun shines onto a surface that is averted from it, the latter lies in its own shadow, and thus a certain ground area also lies in shadow, the so-called cast shadow. The shadow continues until the sun's rays reach the plane on which the surface stands. Since all surfaces which stand on the plane (Earth's surface) vanish on the horizon, all horizontal shadows also vanish on the horizon. Hence the nadir of the sun is also on the horizon in projection.

Theorem: The sun's nadir always lies at the intersecting point between the vanishing traces of

the projected light beam plane and the vanishing plane on which the shadow is cast (in this case, the horizon).

Figure 13.2: Parallel Light

When the solar angle α is parallel to π, this angle remains constant, as does the angle of incidence β. The construction is shown in the drawing.

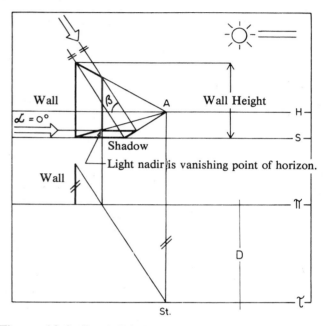

Figure 13.3: Back Light

The sun is unseen behind the observer's back. The object is in the light and so casts a partially visible shadow onto the Earth.

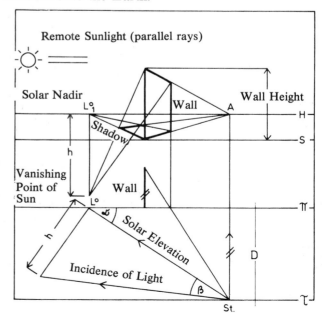

The vanishing point of the sun L^O lies beneath the horizon H—it is determined by St, D, α, and β. h is the distance of the solar vanishing point L^O from the horizon. The solar nadir (L^O_1) lies at the intersection of the vanishing traces of the sun and the Earth's surface (cf. Theorem to Figure 13.1).

Figure 13.4a/b: Canopies

Figure 13.4a. The solar nadir L^O_2 lies at the intersection of the projected light beam plane and the vanishing plane on which the shadow is cast. The projection of the sun is horizontal, like the canopy, which lies in its own shadow. Umbra shadow is cast on the wall (counter light).

Figure 13.4b. The sun's vanishing point is determined by α, β, St, and D. The sun shines down from behind the observer; h from the inverted triangle in ground plan is plotted beneath H, where we find L^O. The surface on which the shadow is cast does not vanish because it runs parallel to π. A is the sole reference point for perspective; thus the solar nadir is "frozen."

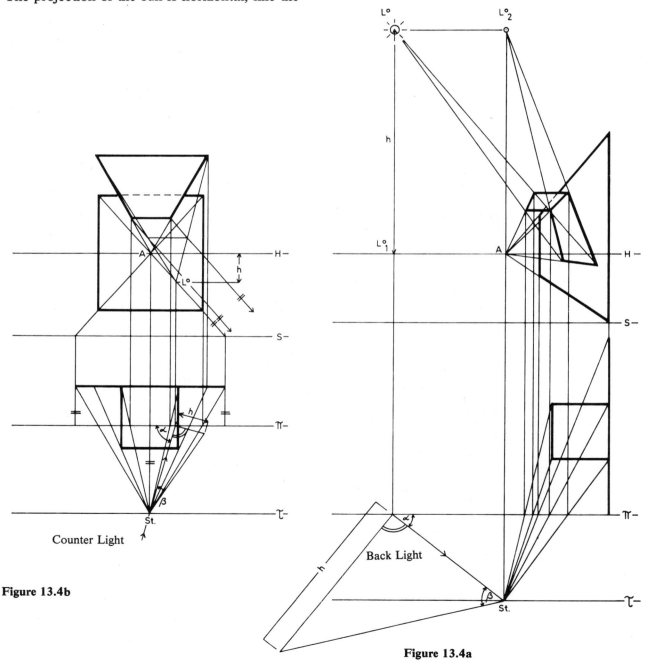

Counter Light

Figure 13.4b

Back Light

Figure 13.4a

Figure 13.5: Counter Light (L^o above H)

L^o_2 lies in the vanishing line of the surface onto which the shadow falls and in the perspective perpendicular (projection) between L^o and Fr.

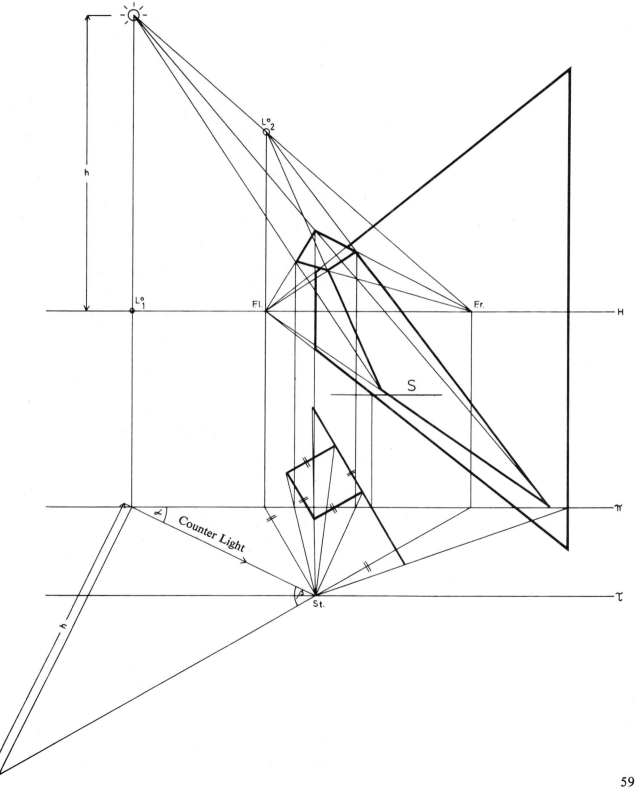

Figure 13.6: Back Light (L^o beneath H)

L^o_2 lies in the vanishing plane of the surface on which the shadow falls and in the extension of the perspective perpendicular (projection) from Fl via L^o.

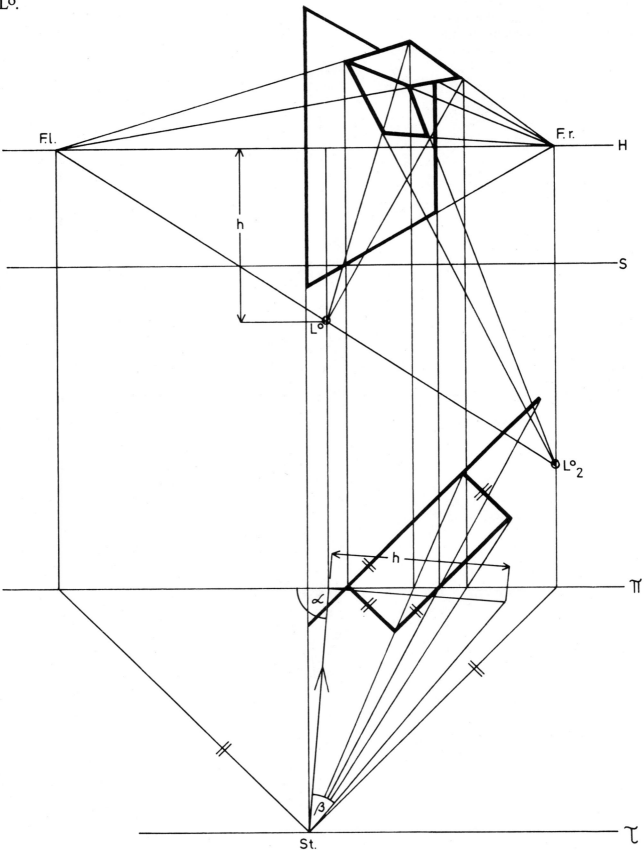

Figure 13.7: Counter Light from L^O

L^O is projected onto the vanishing line of the surface on which the shadow appears. L^O_2 is at the intersection. All lines leaving L^O_2 lie in this plane.

For the shadow cast by the low wall, we use L^O_1, the projection of L^O onto the vanishing line H of the horizontal plane.

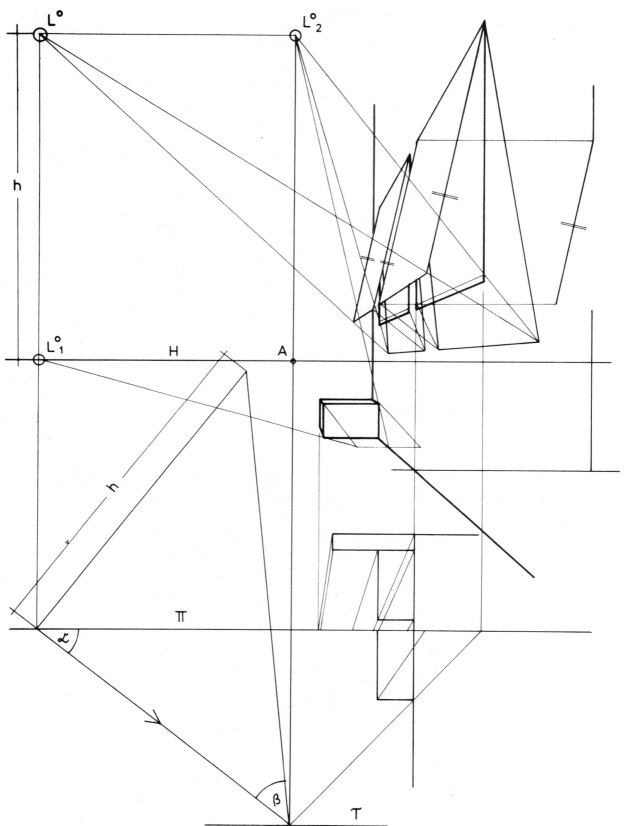

Figure 13.8a: Back Light (Sunblinds)

Since the surface on which the shadow is cast has no vanishing plane, because it runs parallel to π, the nadir angle of the sun remains constant. It runs from L^O to A.

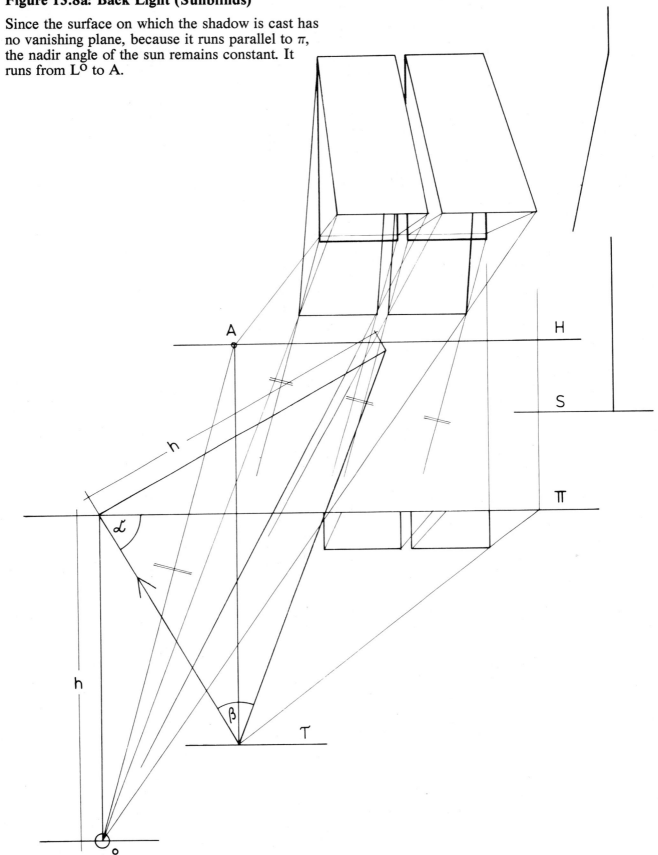

Figure 13.8b shows the freehand drawing of the
shadow as constructed in Figure 13.8a.

Figure 13.9a: Counter Light

L^O_2 lies in the vanishing plane of the surface onto which the shadow falls and in the perspective perpendicular (projection) between L^O and Fr.

For the shadow cast by the low wall, we use L^O_1, the projection of L^O onto the vanishing plane H of the horizon.

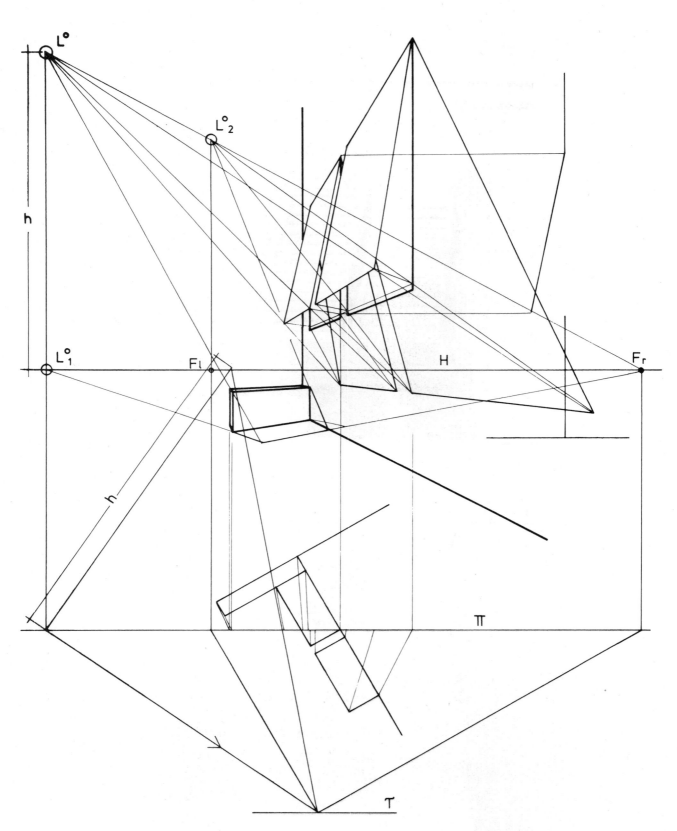

Figure 13.9b is the freehand drawing of the shadow constructed in Figure 13.9a.

Figures 13.10–13.13: Roof Shadows

Figure 13.10.1a: Counter Light

L^o_2 lies in the projection of L^o onto the vanishing line of the roof surface on which the shadow appears. The construction is clearly shown in the drawing.

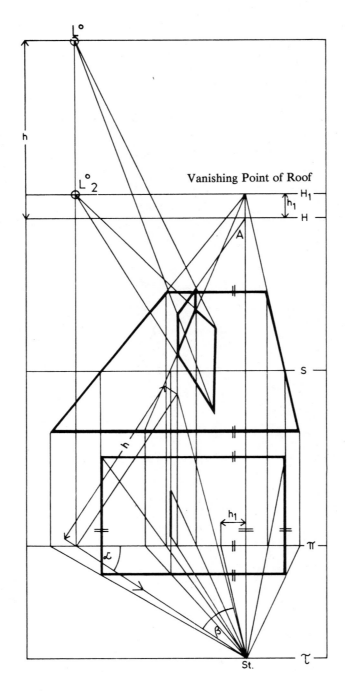

Figure 13.10.1b shows the applied roof shadow from Figure 13.10.1a. L^o_1 has been used for the ground shadow.

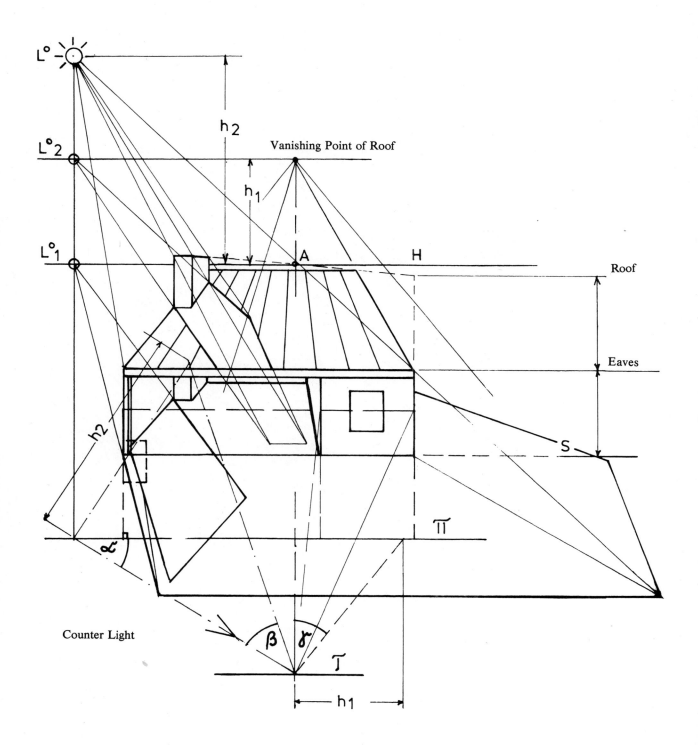

Figure 13.10.1c shows the freehand drawing of
the shadow as constructed in Figure 13.10.1b.

Figure 13.10.2. The sun travels parallel to π and/or τ. The basic rays of the sun run parallel to H. The sunbeams run parallel to β.

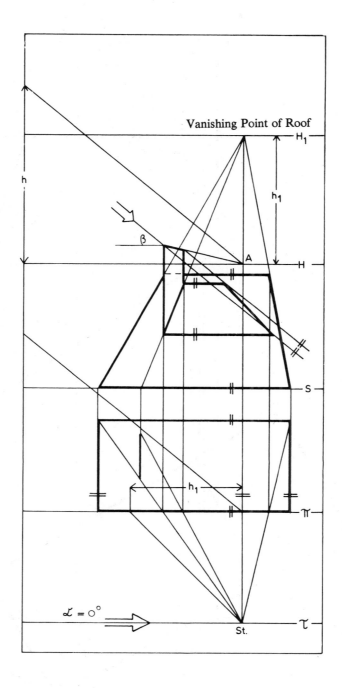

Figure 13.11. The path of the sun is parallel to π and/or τ. β in front elevation is constant. The basic rays of the sun run invisibly parallel to H. $\alpha = 0$.

The pitch of the roof causes the visible basic rays of the sun to run towards the basic vanishing point Fr.

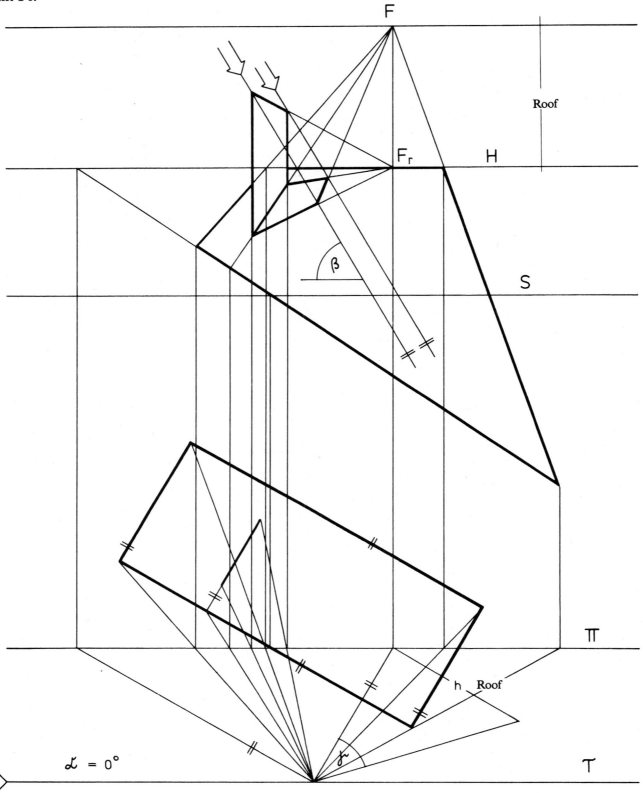

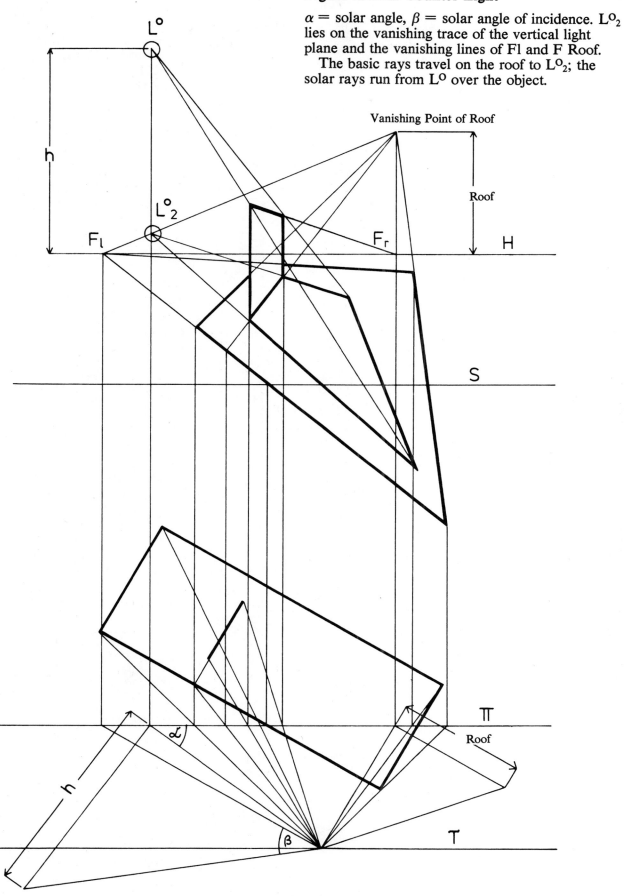

Figure 13.12a: Counter Light

α = solar angle, β = solar angle of incidence. L^O_2 lies on the vanishing trace of the vertical light plane and the vanishing lines of Fl and F Roof.

The basic rays travel on the roof to L^O_2; the solar rays run from L^O over the object.

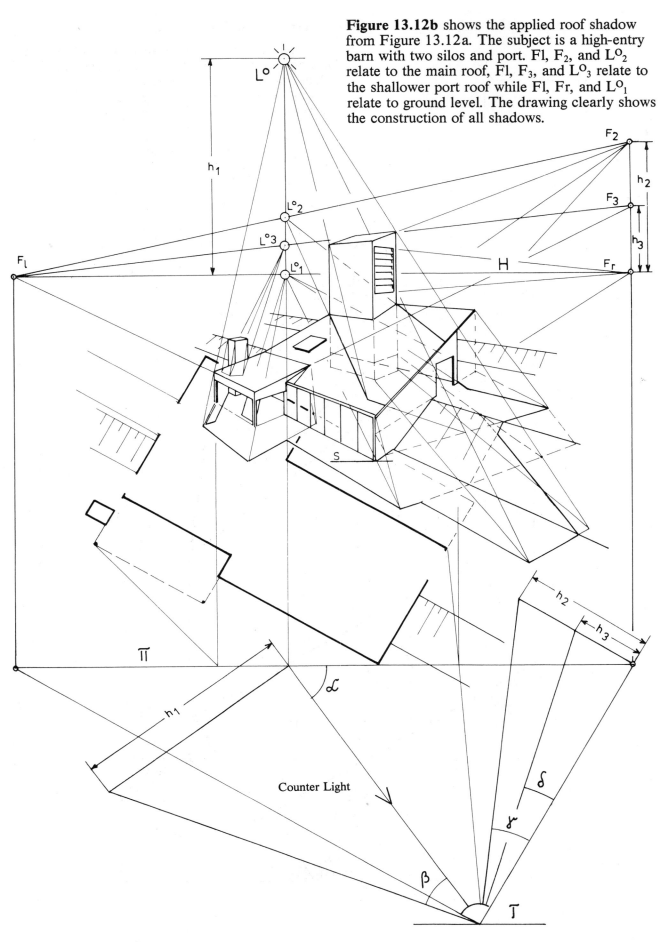

Figure 13.12b shows the applied roof shadow from Figure 13.12a. The subject is a high-entry barn with two silos and port. Fl, F_2, and L^O_2 relate to the main roof, Fl, F_3, and L^O_3 relate to the shallower port roof while Fl, Fr, and L^O_1 relate to ground level. The drawing clearly shows the construction of all shadows.

Counter Light

Figure 13.12c shows the freehand drawing of all shadows constructed in Figure 13.12b.

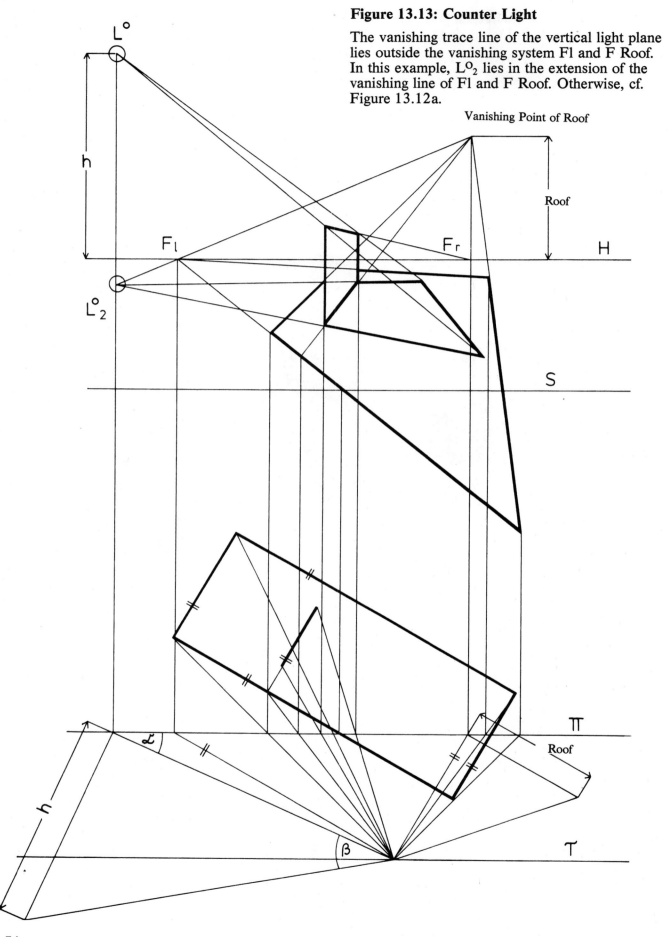

Figure 13.13: Counter Light

The vanishing trace line of the vertical light plane lies outside the vanishing system Fl and F Roof. In this example, L^o_2 lies in the extension of the vanishing line of Fl and F Roof. Otherwise, cf. Figure 13.12a.

Vanishing Point of Roof

Roof

L^o

h

F_l

L^o_2

F_r

H

S

Roof

h

$\mathcal{L}$

π

Roof

β

T

Figure 13.14: Back Light (Tower with Overhanging Roof)

Two shadow constructions are required:

1. Shadow on a wall that is parallel to π.
2. Shadow on a wall that is perpendicular to π.

1. Since the wall does not vanish, all the sun's basic rays run parallel to the path L^O-A in the perspective image. As usual, the sunlight travels to L^O via the underside of the roof slab.

2. The surface perpendicular to π has the vanishing point A.

   The basic rays of the sun must lie in the vanishing line in which A also lies. The vanishing trace of the horizontal light plane intersects the vanishing line of A at L^O_2.

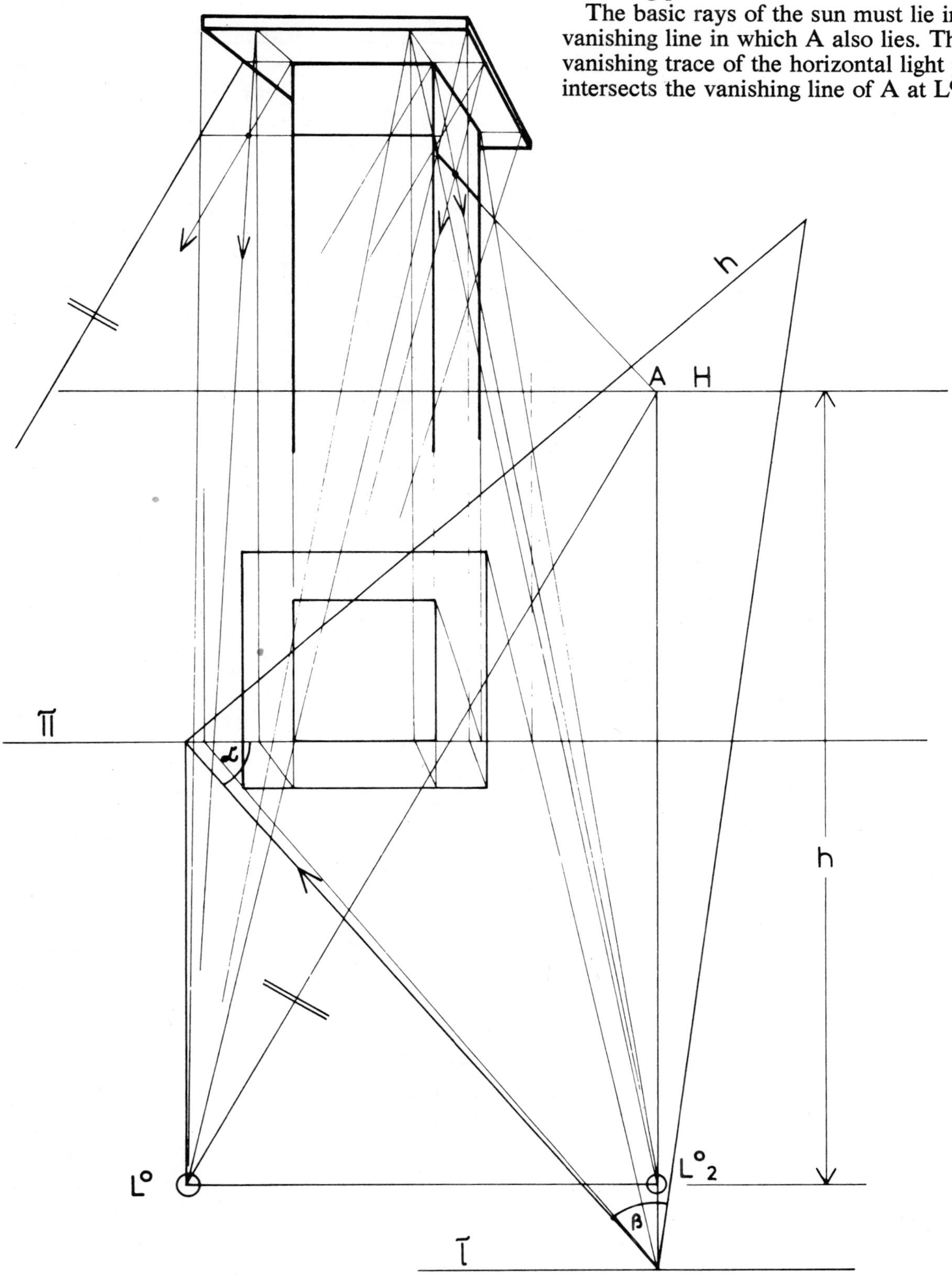

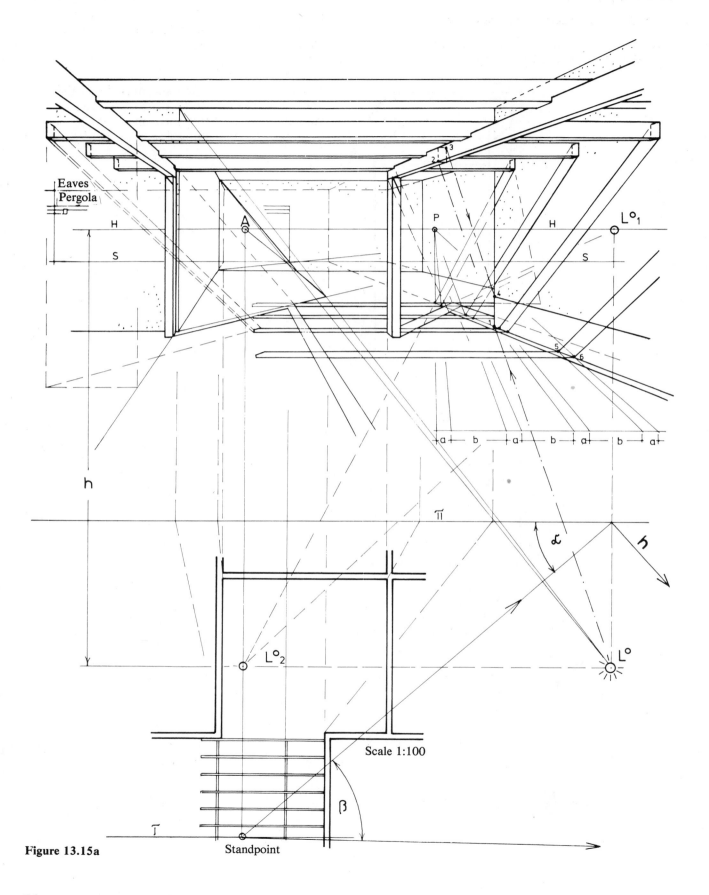

Figure 13.15a

Eaves
Pergola

H

S

A

P

H   L°₁

S

3
2

4

5
6

├ a ┤├ b ┤├ a ┤├ b ┤├ a ┤├ b ┤├ a ┤

h

π

α

ƛ

L°₂

L°

Scale 1:100

β

τ

Standpoint

76

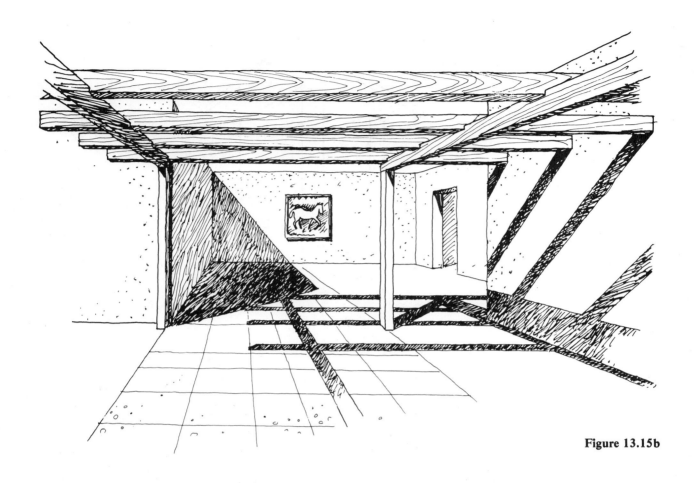

Figure 13.15b

Figure 13.15a: Back Light (Pergola and Forecourt)

This is a central perspective (cf. Figure 5.1a— ground plan with τ and π, front elevation with S and H).

α, β, and h determine the position of the sun L^O. L^O_1 is the base point in the vanishing line H for all shadows that fall on the horizontal plane. L^O_2 is the basic vanishing point for the beams whose shadows fall on the right-hand wall (cf. Figure 13.14).

An auxiliary line is drawn from L^O through the corner of the right-hand wall (point 1) to the underside of the pergola beam (point 2). The perspective cross section of this beam gives us point 3. A sunbeam from point 3 to L^O gives us point 4, and this provides the shadow height of the same beam on the wall. The intersecting points of the pergola on the wall are joined to L^O_2. These shadow edges intersect the wall's edge at ground level, and the pergola's horizontal shadow passes through these points. The left-hand end of the beams can be easily seen from the drawing. Here L^O_1 must be used as a guide. To find points 5 and 6, we use the perspective division method (Figure 10.3) with the aid of a random point P in H.

From P we plot lines through the visible points in the wall's edge and its extension to any desired base line. We obtain the rhythmical divisions of a and b. The same rhythm is continued to the right, and the resulting points are traced back to P when we obtain the points 5 and 6 through which the wall and ground shadows pass.

Figure 13.15b shows the freehand drawing based on Figure 13.15a.

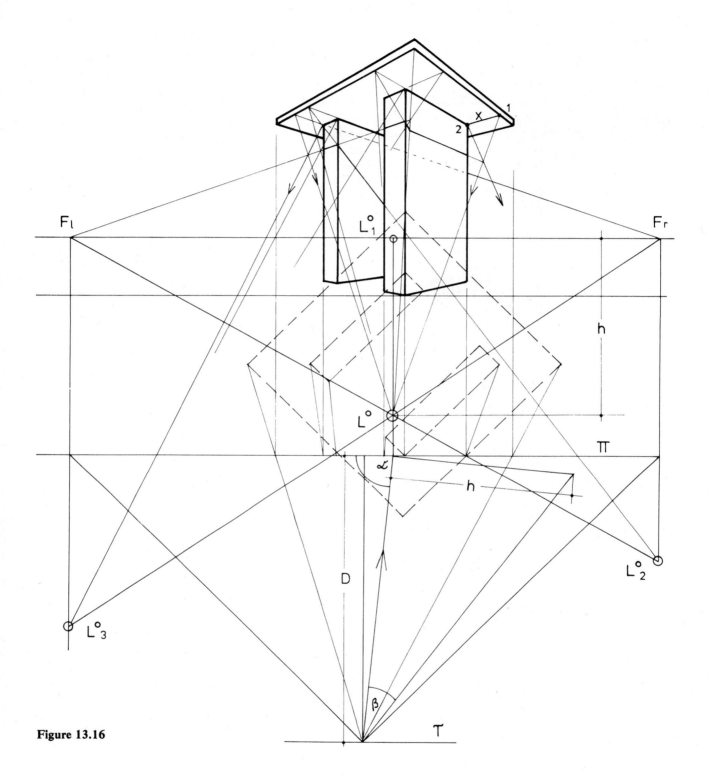

Figure 13.16

Figure 13.16: Back Light (Main Works of a Signalbox)

The construction of the dual vanishing point perspective can be seen from the drawing. h is determined by α and β. With h we obtain L^O. The vanishing lines of Fr and Fl are the first geometric locations of L^O_2 and L^O_3, the basic vanishing points of the sun on the vertical faces of the structure.

The second geometric location for L^O_2 lies on the extension of the vanishing trace of the light plane from Fl through L^O.

The second geometric location for L^O_3 lies similarly on the extension of Fr through L^O.

Remarks: The foregoing exercises are all based on the same premises. The sun must be integrated into the perspective system. An oblique surface vanishes in a given line on which its vanishing point lies—e.g., Fr. A perpendicular to that surface—e.g., x—will cast its shadow onto that surface from point 1 to L^O and from point 2 to the base point of the Sun L^O_2. The line 2, L^O_2 lies in the surface.

L^O_2 lies in the vanishing point of L^O to Fl because the line x also vanishes to Fl.

Note the relative interdependence of all vanishing traces.

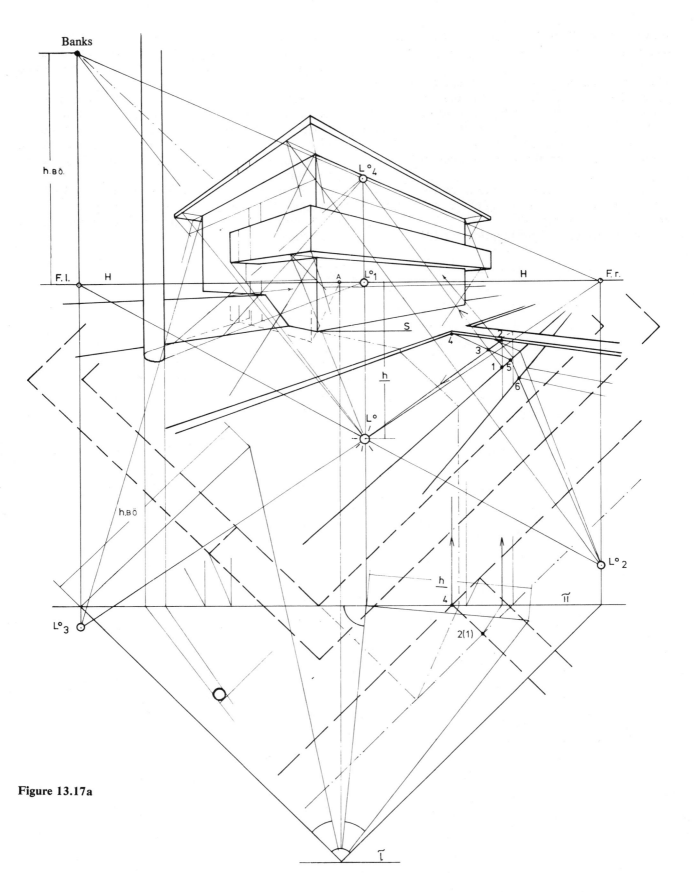

Figure 13.17a

80

Figure 13.17b

Figure 13.17: Boathouse

This illustration is based directly on the construction in Figure 13.16.

There is an added vanishing point for the bank (cf. Figure 13.17a). The solar base point L^O_4 lies on the vanishing trace between F Bank and Fr on the one hand, and on the vanishing trace of the vertical light plane from L^O on the other.

The umbra shadow of the tree trunk at left vanishes to L^O_4 after aiming for L^O_1 on the terrace.

The cast shadow of the tree on the wall is clearly visible, offset by the balcony.

The shadow of the jetty on the bank, the quay, and the water requires a special auxiliary construction:

Points 1 and 2 are taken from ground plan.

Point 2 goes to L^O; point 1 to L^O_4. We obtain point 3, which is joined up to point 4 and projected down to the break of the bank (point 5).

The shadow on the quay goes to L^O_2. We obtain point 6. The extension of point 6 and Fl gives us the outline of the shadow on the water. The right-hand shadow line of the jetty is constructed in similar fashion.

Figure 13.17b shows the freehand drawing with added detail. The construction is shown in Figure 13.17a.

Figure 13.18a: Arch Shadows (Back Light)

α, β, and h give L^O below the horizon H. Since the surface on which the shadow falls has no vanishing point, the projection of the solar shadow L^O to A is constant. The arch in this example consists of a floorless shell against a wall.

The arch is constructed by means of the breakthrough method.

From K_1 and B_1 we draw the parallels to the base angle of the sun L^O-A. The sun's rays are drawn from impost point K and base point B to L^O. The parallelogram 1, 2, K_1, and B_1 is the umbra shadow of the upright intrados of the shell. M_1 is the center of the circular shadow which intersects the innermost arch at 3. The auxiliary point K_2 on the impost line is determined from the ground plan and provides us with an intermediate arc on which point 4 lies. A solar projection, the parallel to L^O-A through K_2, gives the point KS. The arch from KS about M_3 intersects the auxiliary circle at point 4. Point 5 is the tangential point on the outer arch: the tangent is a parallel to the solar projection L^O-A. Points 3, 4, and 5, when joined together, give the edge of the shadow on the inner arches.

Figure 13.18b shows a door of the Abbey at Essen-Werden, Germany. This is a floorless shell built against a wall. The ground shadow is constructed with L^O_1 and L^O—construction corresponds with Figure 13.18a.

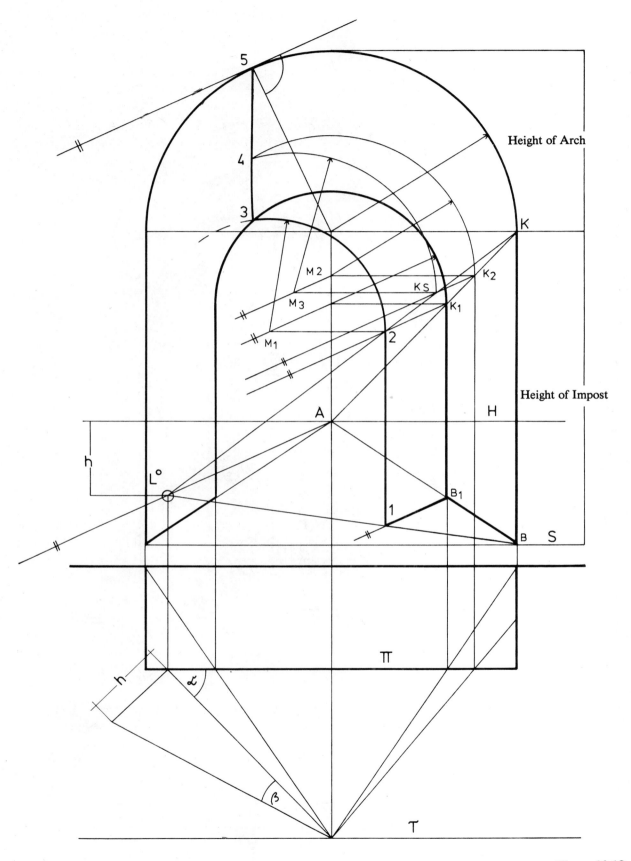

Height of Arch

Height of Impost

Figure 13.18a

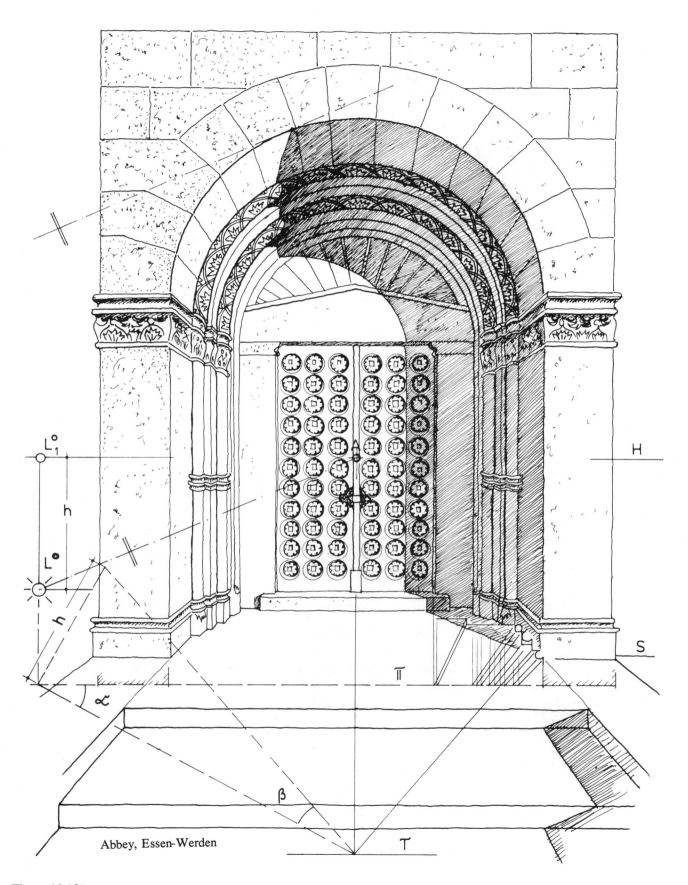

L_1^o

h

L^o

h

α

β

π

T

H

S

Abbey, Essen-Werden

Figure 13.18b

Figure 13.19a: Open Arch Against a Wall (Counter Light)

Construction of the shell (cf. Figure 12.1.5, Bridge).

L^O_2 is the base point of the sun on the wall and lies in the vanishing trace of the horizontal light plane on the one hand and in the vanishing trace of the wall through A. The lines with which the ellipse is constructed lie perpendicular to the wall and serve to construct the shadow on the wall.

Example: Light rays L^O via point 1 and L^O_2 via point 2 lead to point 3 of the elliptical shadow.

Figure 13.19b. Example: Atrium with palm tree.

In this drawing L^O_1 has been used to construct the floor shadow. Otherwise, it is as constructed in Figure 13.19a.

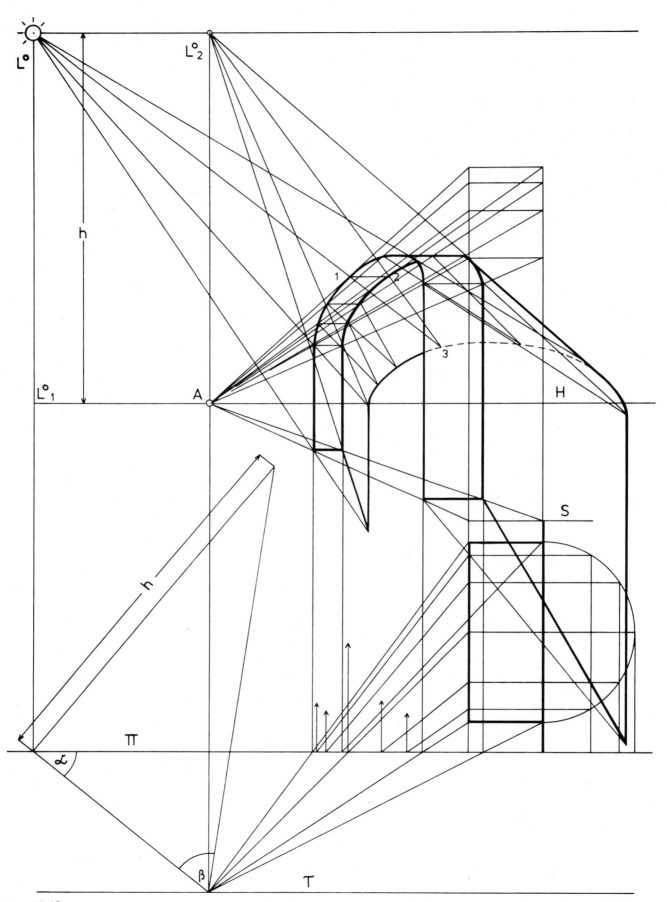

Figure 13.19a

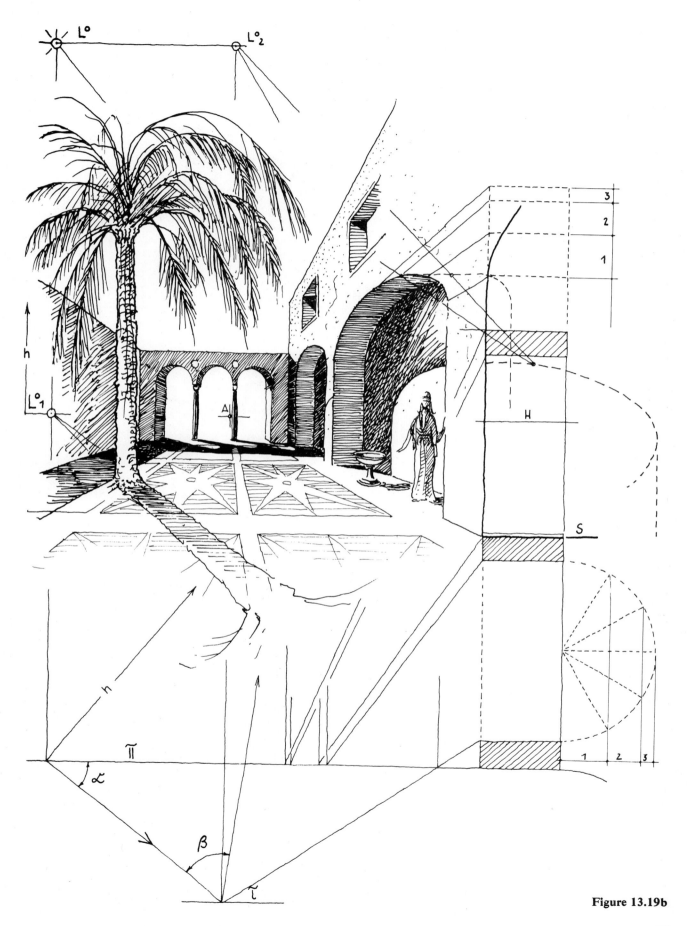

Figure 13.19b

Figure 13.20a: Freestanding Arch

The construction of the shell is shown in the drawing (cf. Circle in Perspective, Figure 12.1.5).

The cast shadow starts beneath the shell at tangent points 1 to L^O_3. Point 2 serves as an example for other intermediate points. The connection of 2 to 3 which leads on to L^O_3 is level with the arch. The vanishing line from point 3 to Fr is the first geometric location for shadow point 4. The sunbeam from 2 to L^O provides the second geometric location for point 4. The ground shadow runs from point 6 to L^O_1. Point 5 is the point of intersection between the ground shadow and the curved shadow in the arch.

From points 7 and 8, the ground shadow runs elliptical to L^O_1. No further construction is required here, since most of the shadow is invisible.

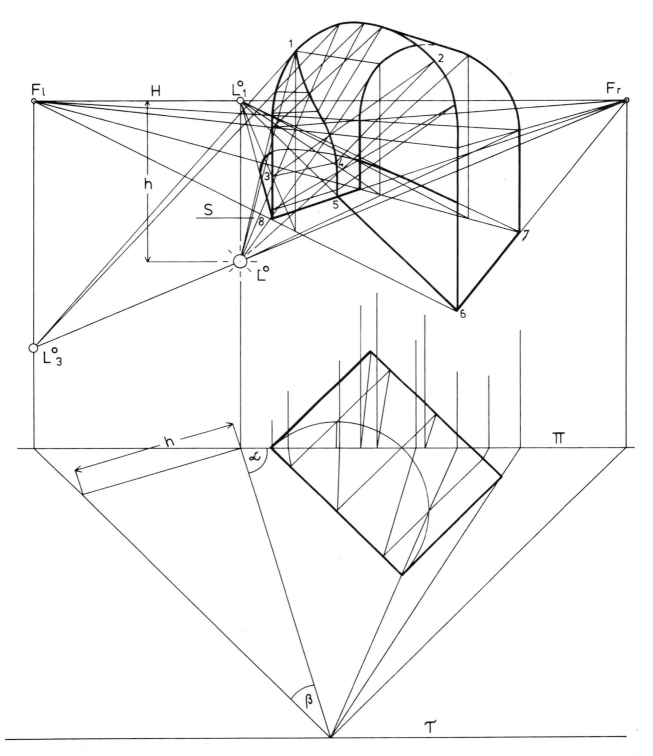

Figure 13.20a

Figure 13.20b: Gateway of an Old Castle

The construction is taken from the preceding archway (Figure 13.20a). The two sundials are a particular feature.

The sundial shadows which indicate the hour are different because the walls are at right angles to each other.

The sundial scales have to be matched to each other.

The position of the sundials is constructed from the ground plan using the breakthrough method. Only one sundial need be described here.

The hand is perpendicular to the wall and vanishes to Fr.

FS is the nadir of the hand,
SP is the point of the hand,
ZW is the root of the pointer,
SS is the end of the hand's shadow,
ZS is the pointer shadow.

FS is vanished to L^o_3 (projection) and SP to L^o.

The point of intersection is the end of the hand's shadow SS. The connection of pointer root ZW and SS provides the pointer shadow, which in turn shows the time of day on the scale.

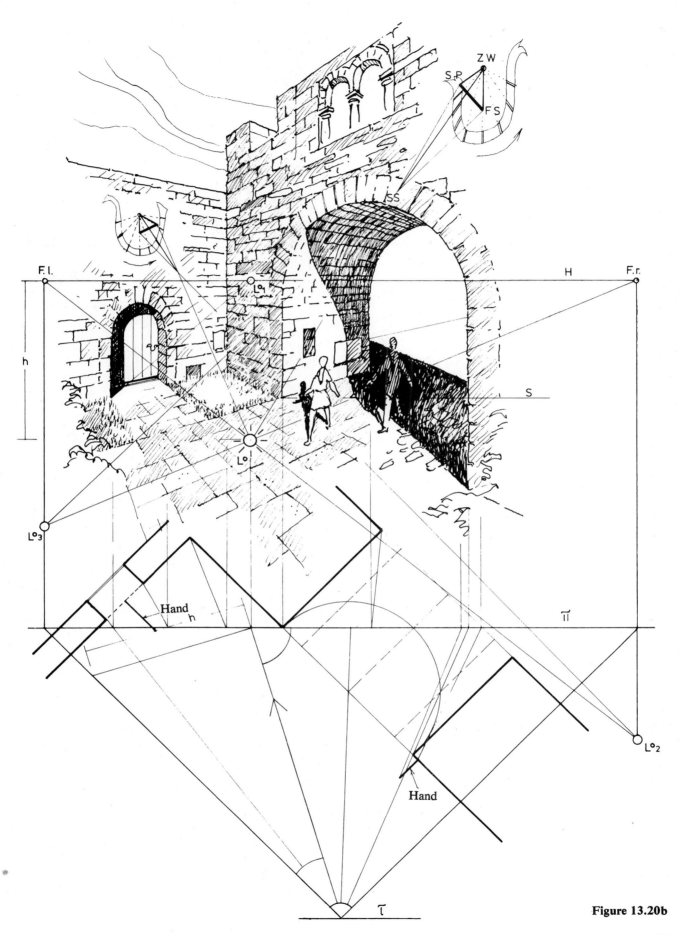

Figure 13.20b

14. Central Shadow

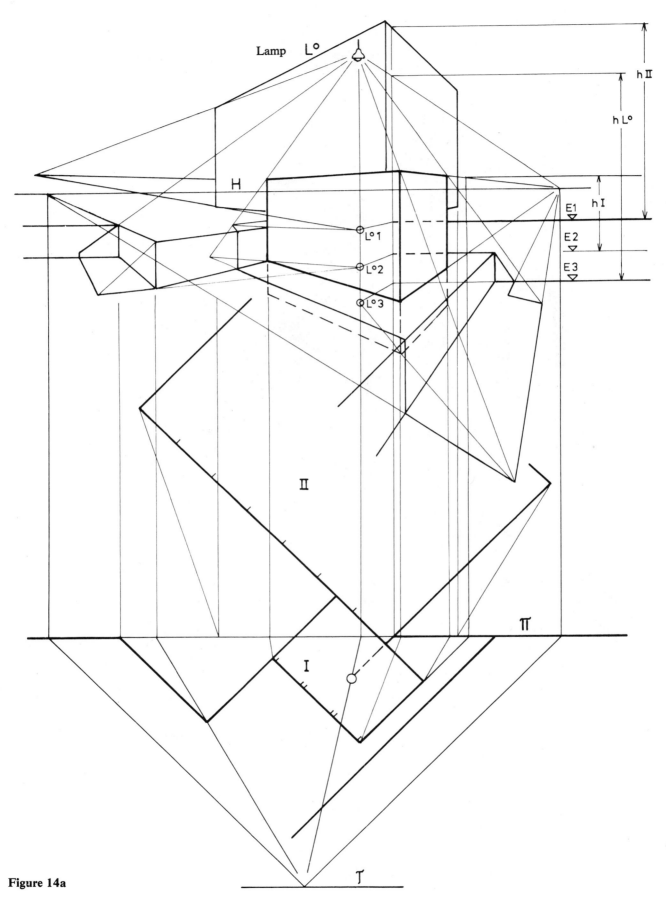

Figure 14a

Natural darkness is illuminated by artificial lighting, and we only see what the artificial light actually reaches (Figure 14.a).

Quite apart from purely functional aspects, architecture can play an essential part in the lighting of spaces and the illumination of particular objects.

Nevertheless, it is rare to see illustrations of lighting effects in architects' studios (paintings, photos, or designs), and so our example should provide a guide to the theory of central shadow.

Factory buildings and warehouses are illuminated by an outside lamp which creates areas of light, shade, and cast shadow.

The lamp throws its light over the buildings and yards. Each level has its own lamp nadir, which is a perspective location on that level in the projection of the lamp. Sunlight is different in that it has but one nadir on the horizon for all planes— L^o_1.

The construction of perspective and shadows can be seen from the drawing.

Figure 14.b. The freely drawn illustration is identical with the construction on the opposite page.

15. Reflections—Vertical

Figure 15.1. The mirror lies in π and in H-S. The object lies at distance a in front of π. The reflection is constructed in ground plan with a behind π.

In front elevation, object and reflection are constructed as if they were two objects.

Figure 15.2. The mirror is perpendicular to π and vanishes in front elevation to A. In ground plan, the reflection of the object (left) is drawn and handled with the object in front elevation as if it were an object as well.

Figure 15.3. In this example, the mirror is an affinity axis which reflects by vertical projection. The reflection in ground plan is handled in front elevation as if it were an object like the object itself, which also appears in front elevation. The reflection has a new vanishing point because of the change in attitude.

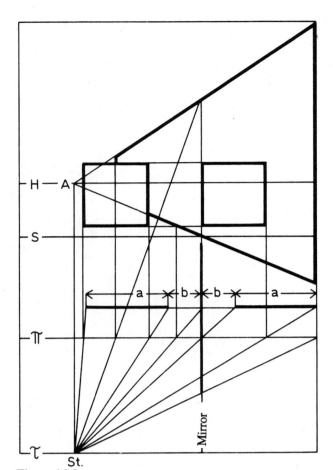

Figure 15.2

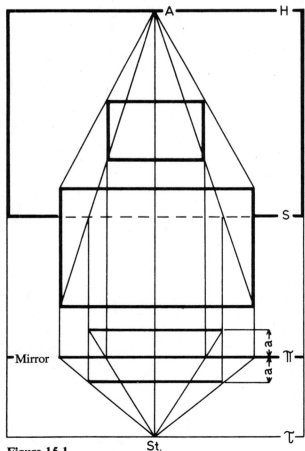

Figure 15.1

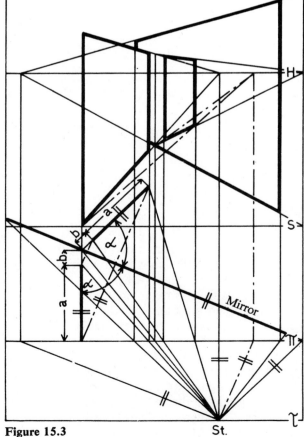

Figure 15.3

Figure 15.4a. The inclined mirror reflects the corner of a room that lies behind τ. Because of affinity, the angles of the walls are changed in the mirror, and each new angle has its own vanishing point.

Figure 15.5a. The wall of a narrow room consists of a mirror in π. The reflection of the rear wall in ground plan behind τ is visible in front elevation. The room appears larger.

Figure 15.6a. The room lies oblique to π. Because of the reflection of the room in ground plan, the right-hand rear corner of the room becomes visible in front elevation.

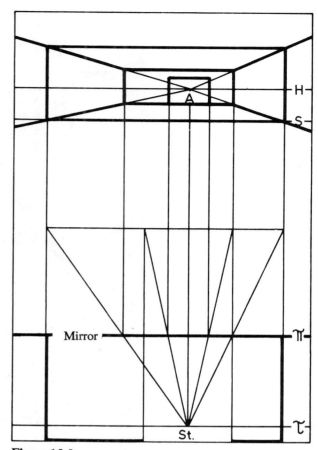

Figure 15.5a

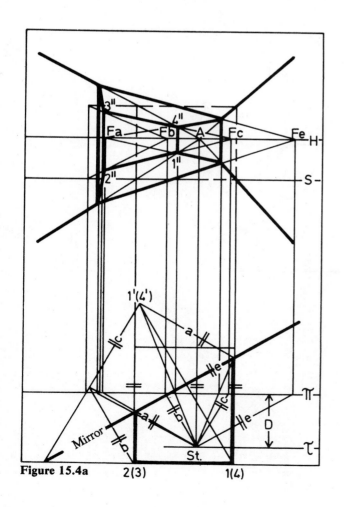

Figure 15.4a

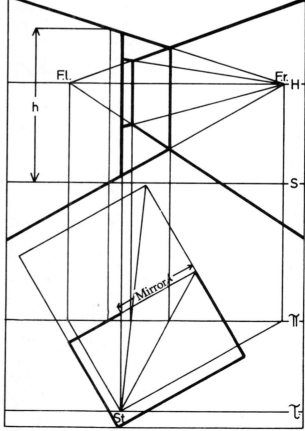

Figure 15.6a

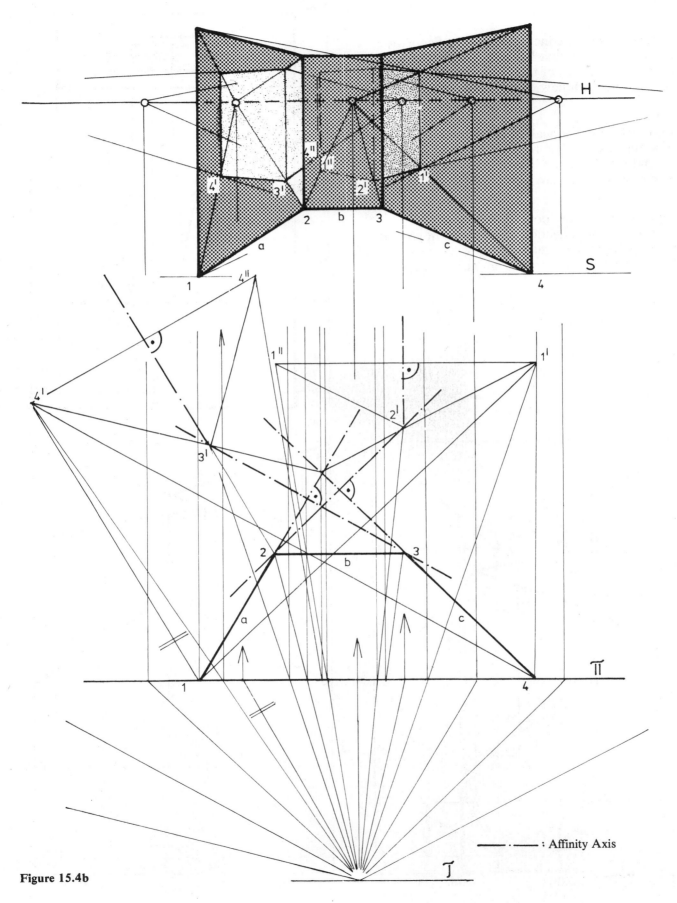

Figure 15.4b

—·—·— : Affinity Axis

Figure 15.4b. There are three mirrors—a, b, and c. In mirror a, we set up an affinity axis on which point 3 is reflected. This becomes 3'. Now where is point 3' in the reflection? The vanishing point for the perspective line from 2 to 3' is located in ground plan. If we now draw a line parallel to 2-3' through the standpoint to π, we obtain an intersecting point on π whose projection in H is the vanishing point for the perspective line from 2 to 3'. The second geometric location for 3' is found by the breakthrough method.

4' is also found via the affinity axis 1-2. The straight line 1-4' runs parallel to 2-3' in ground plan, so 1-4' has the same vanishing point as 2-3'. We obtain this point in the picture by the breakthrough method. 2-3' now becomes the affinity axis for the reflection of point 4'. 4" is found just as rapidly: we obtain it by using the vanishing point and breakthrough methods. The vertical sides of the mirror pass through image points 3', 4', and 4". The top reflected edges of the mirrors are obtained with vanishing lines.

No reflection can be seen in mirror b.

In mirror c, point 1 or a part of mirror a is reflected through the affinity axis 4-3.

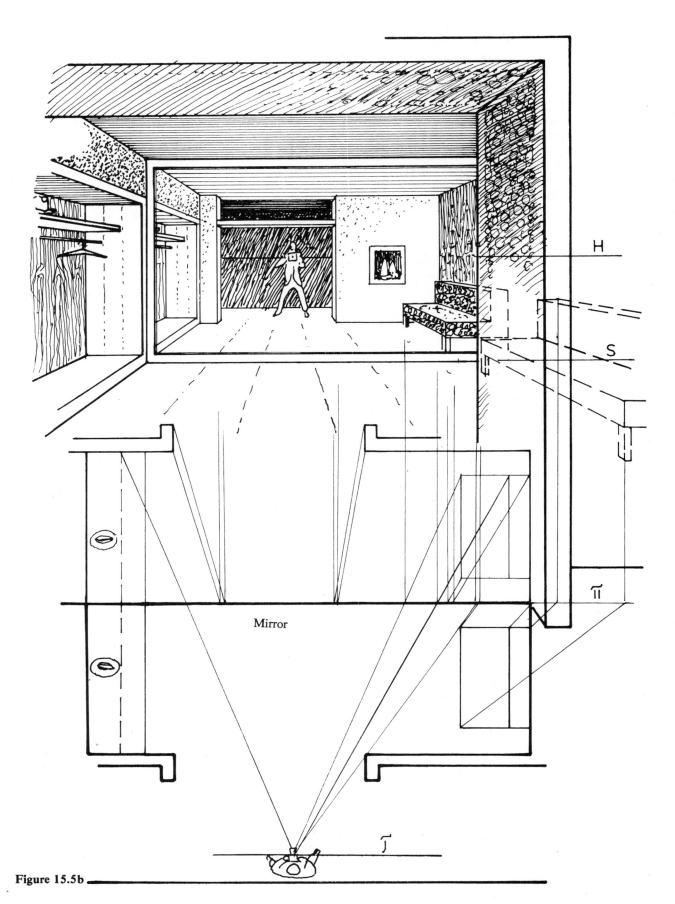

H

S

Ⅱ

Mirror

Ⅰ

Figure 15.5b

98

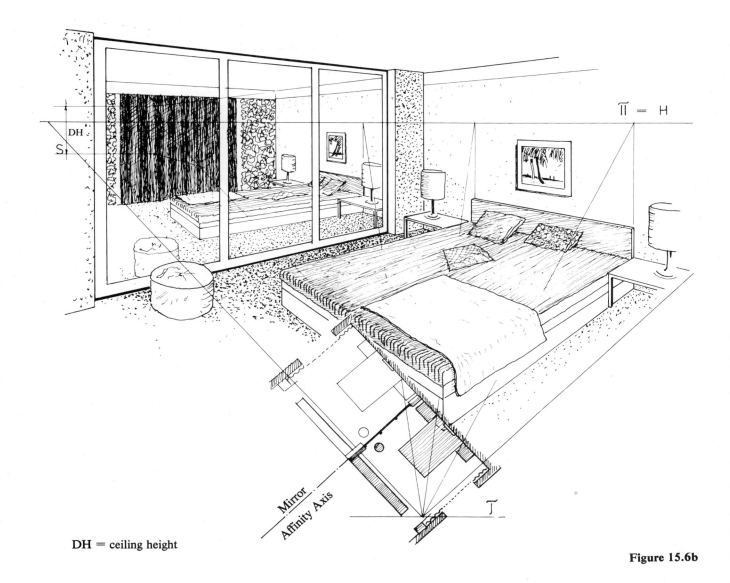

$\overline{\Pi} = H$

DH

S

Mirror
Affinity Axis

$\overline{\top}$

DH = ceiling height

Figure 15.6b

Figure 15.5b. The wall of a narrow room consists of a mirror in π.

The reflection of the rear wall in ground plan behind τ is visible in front elevation, as are the sofa, wall picture, and photographer who stands in τ. The wardrobe is visible twice, in the room and in the mirror.

The mirror has 2 functions:

1. it serves as a wardrobe mirror; and
2. it enlarges the otherwise small room optically and architecturally.

Figure 15.6b. The room lies oblique to π. The reflection makes parts of the room visible which would not otherwise be seen at a glance. The picture plane is far away from the ground plan in this example, making the perspective image much larger.

Constructed using the vanishing point and breakthrough method.

16. Reflections—Horizontal

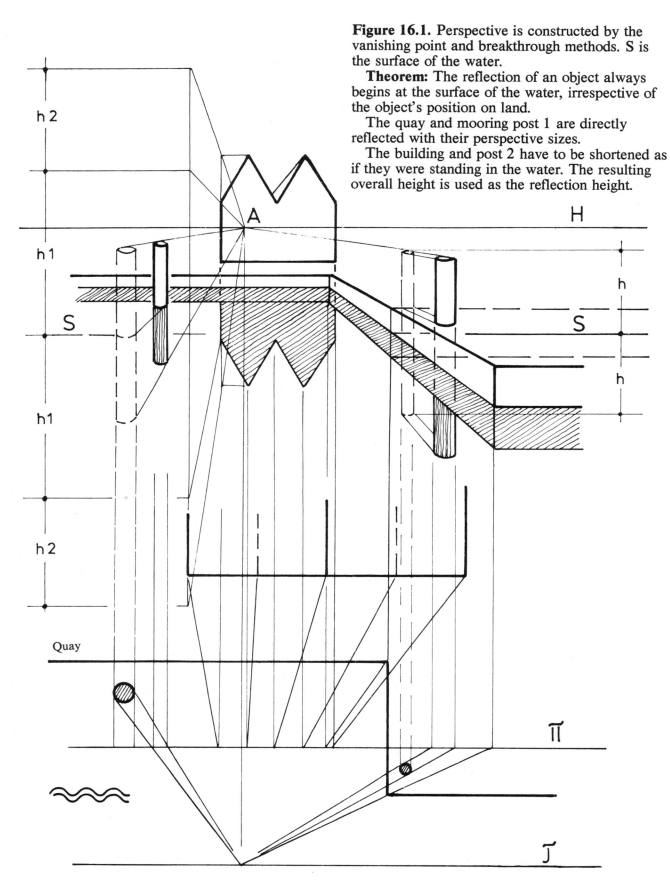

Figure 16.1. Perspective is constructed by the vanishing point and breakthrough methods. S is the surface of the water.

Theorem: The reflection of an object always begins at the surface of the water, irrespective of the object's position on land.

The quay and mooring post 1 are directly reflected with their perspective sizes.

The building and post 2 have to be shortened as if they were standing in the water. The resulting overall height is used as the reflection height.

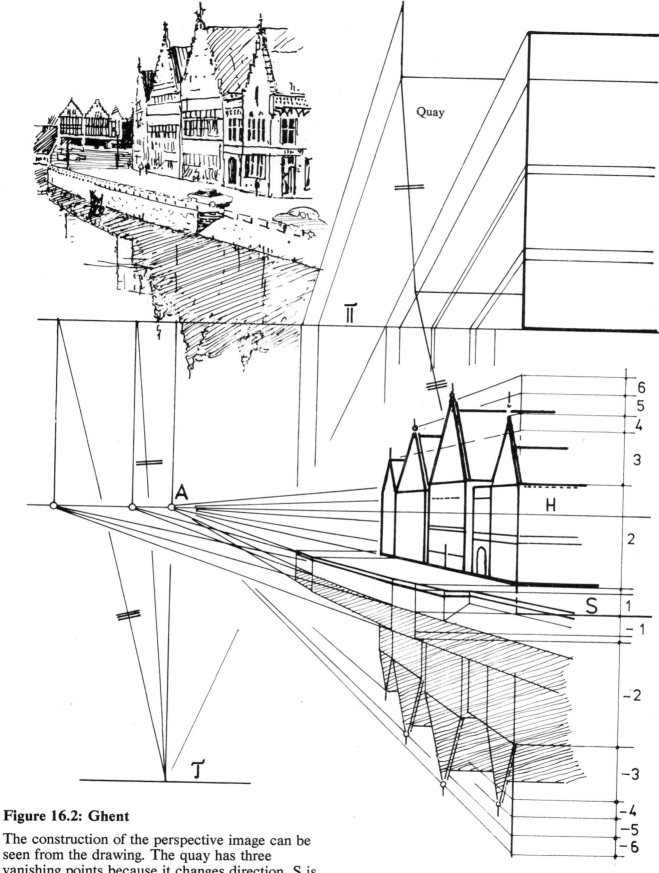

Figure 16.2: Ghent

The construction of the perspective image can be seen from the drawing. The quay has three vanishing points because it changes direction. S is the trace line on the surface of the water; from here, all positive heights for the merchants' houses are measured and then plotted downward to the reflection as negative heights.

This is done from the front edge of the first house because it lies in π.

The sketch is freely drawn.

Figure 16.3a: Quay with Building and Tower

The perspective picture is drawn in the ground plan to save space, although this is not recommended for complex objects. There is also a side elevation, which is not strictly necessary. There are sufficient elevations. The trace line lies on the water level and is also the picture plane π. Once again, the construction of the vanishing points has been used for sloping surfaces. The pitch angle for all roofs is α.

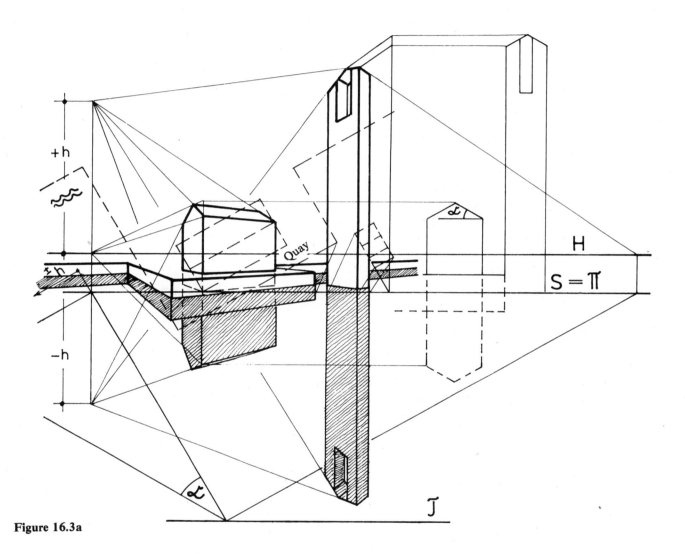

Figure 16.3a

Figure 16.3b: Reflection Constructed from Plan Opposite

The illustration has been freely sketched and detailed.

Figure 16.3b

17. Oblique Picture Plane

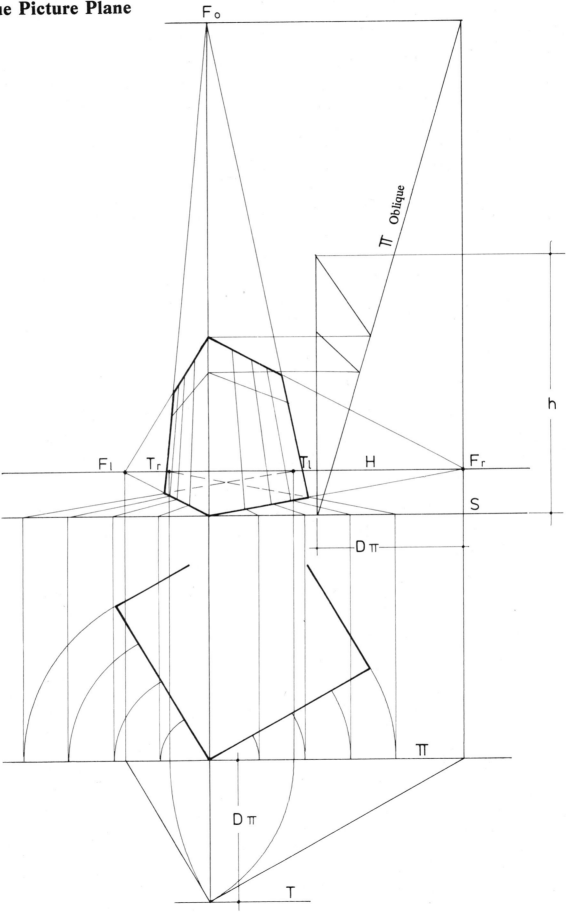

Figure 17.1a

17.1 Worm's-Eye View

Figure 17.1a. The inclination of the picture plane is determined in the side elevation. The sides of a high-rise building have two vanishing points in ground plan by whose projection we obtain Fl and Fr in H. The eye follows the vertical sides of the building up to a trace point on the oblique picture plane. This trace point is horizontally projected onto the main sightline, and we obtain the vanishing point Fo for the vertical corners of the building. The front corner of the building goes—in side elevation—through the intersection point of S, Dπ, and the inclined picture plane. The breakthrough method was used for building heights in side elevation, while the component point process was used for depths in ground plan.

Figures 17.1b, c, and d are all illustrations constructed on the basis of the principle shown in Figure 17.1a. These are freely drawn examples prepared without need of ground plans.

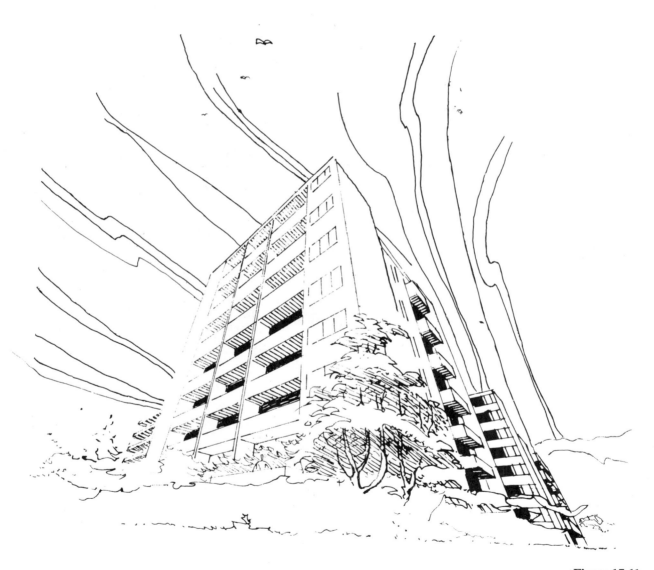

Figure 17.1b

Figure 17.1c

Figure 17.1d

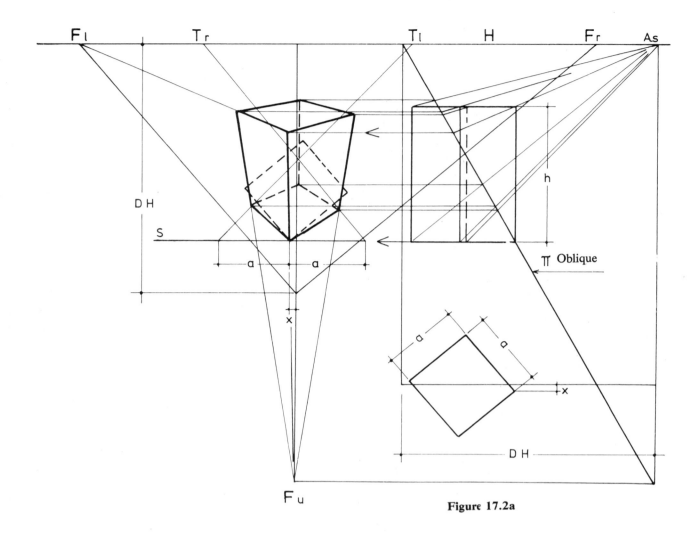

Figure 17.2a

17.2 Bird's-Eye View

Figure 17.2a. In this construction, there is no conventional ground plan to determine vanishing points Fl and Fr. These vanishing points are located by DH and the angles of the prism (shortcut method).

From the side elevation, we first need the inclined picture plane with DH and the projection from eyepoint As with which Fu is found; second, the height of the prism with the point of intersection in π.

The whole form of the prism in side elevation is not absolutely essential.

The perspective image can now be constructed with the component point process and the three existing vanishing points.

Figure 17.2b. A sketch is shown in place of the ground plan, and represents a view of a market square from a church tower. The basic forms of the buildings are cut-off pyramids turned on their heads (cf. Figure 17.2a).

Figure 17.2b

18. Picture Plane Parallel to Ground Plan

Stairwell

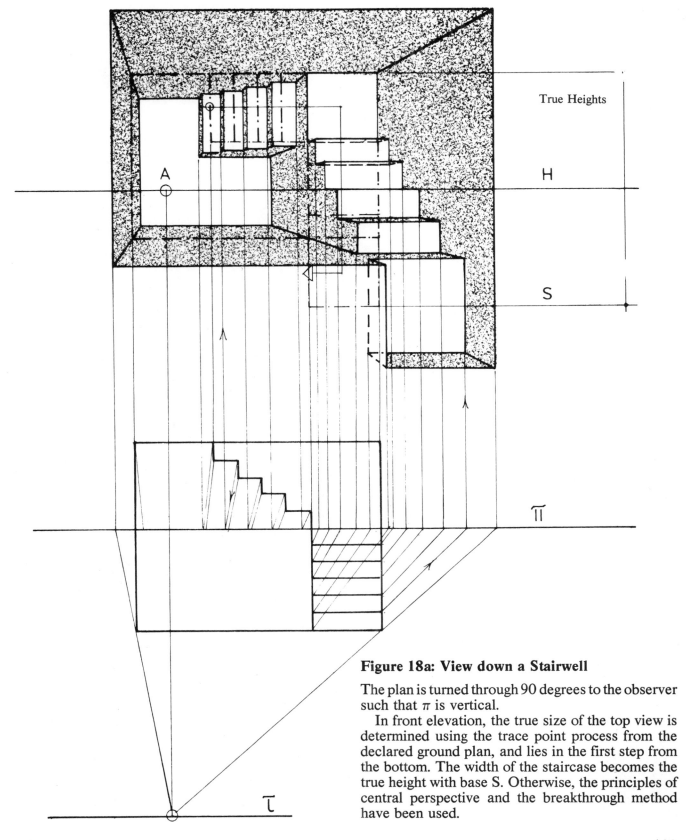

True Heights

H

A

S

π

τ

Figure 18a: View down a Stairwell

The plan is turned through 90 degrees to the observer such that π is vertical.

In front elevation, the true size of the top view is determined using the trace point process from the declared ground plan, and lies in the first step from the bottom. The width of the staircase becomes the true height with base S. Otherwise, the principles of central perspective and the breakthrough method have been used.

Figure 18b. View from treetops to undergrowth below (bird's-eye view).
Construction as in Figure 18a.

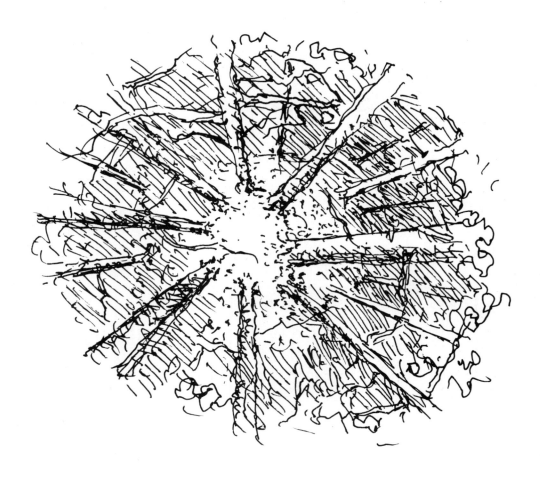

Figure 18c. An old German marketplace (Bernkastel on the Moselle) rises up away from the observer (worm's-eye view). The picture plane is horizontal in ground plane while the buildings lie horizontal in front elevation. Construction as Figure 18a.

19. Fish-Eye Perspective

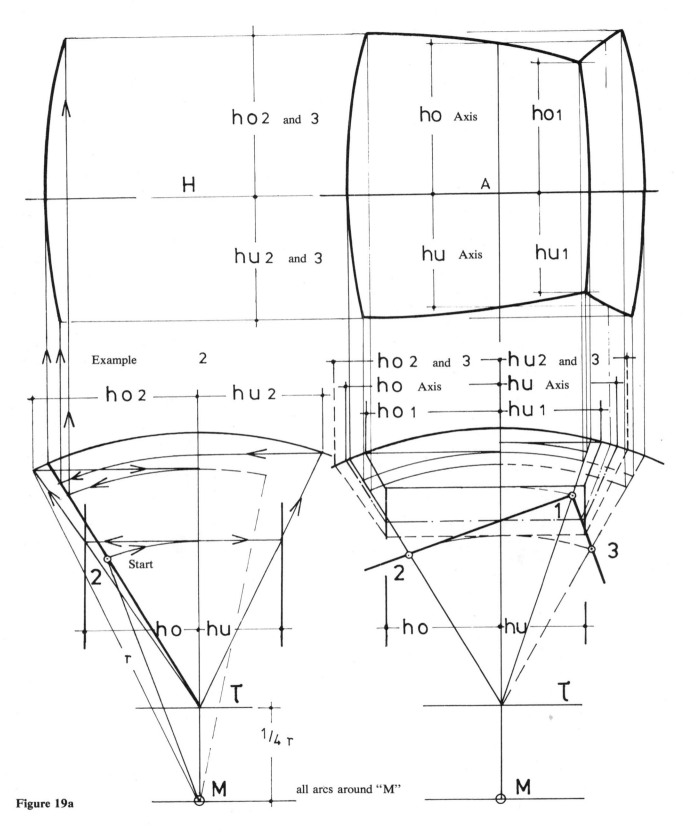

Figure 19a

ho + hu = true heights of walls

Figure 19a. The drawing of illustrations with a spheroid picture plane (fish-eye view) is not common practice (except in photographic reproductions). The effort involved bears no comparison with the effect achieved.

Nevertheless, the theory is scientifically interesting—its thought processes are complex but are still based on fundamental, logical principles. The main principle is the breakthrough method. In this example the object is in front of the picture plane; every single point has to be determined.

The left-hand ground plan shows the course of a point (2) which is turned on its central axis, then pivoted over. We obtain two points in ho and hu. In perspective, the height increases because 2 lies in front of the picture plane. This is why this latter point is extended through τ to the picture plane. Since point 2 in front elevation is the edge of a wall, it has two heights, ho_2 and hu_2. One mean point of this wall edge lies on the horizon, and is projected from ground plan to H. In front elevation, there are three points which—when interconnected—make the straight line of buildings from 2 appear curved. This system of points turns all straight lines into arcs, while center axis and horizon remain straight.

Figure 19b: Apartment Blocks with Pergola

All straight lines bend to the constraints of the spheroid picture plane (fish-eye lens).

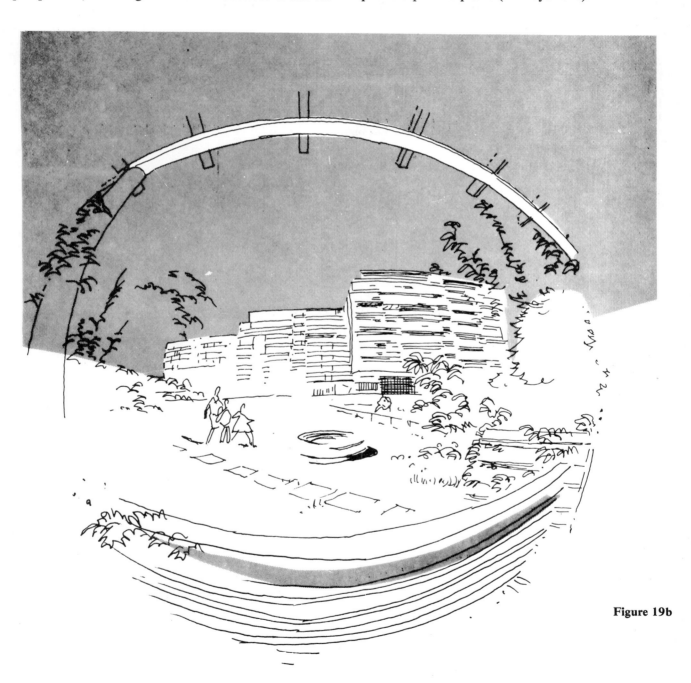

Figure 19b

Key to Abbreviations and Symbols

A	=	eyepoint, vertical above standpoint = central vanishing point
π	=	picture plane determining the size and shape of the picture
D	=	distance (i.e., of observer from picture plane)
Std.pkt.	=	standpoint in τ
τ	=	standing or vanishing plane
M	=	center of circle
H	=	horizon
h	=	true object heights and true sight heights above or below horizon as seen from the eyepoint or vanishing point
Fl	=	vanishing point at left on horizon
Fr	=	vanishing point at right on horizon
Tl	=	component point left, appears at right on horizon
Tr	=	component point right, appears at left on horizon
S	=	trace line
$\parallel$	=	parallel
$\perp$	=	perpendicular
α, β, γ	=	angles
$\measuredangle$	=	angle sign
$\rightarrow$	=	projection
L^o	=	solar vanishing point (Lux)
L^o_1	=	solar nadir on horizon in the vanishing trace of the vertical light plane
$L^o_{2.3.4}$	=	vanishing trace of the sun on other planes
$\dot{\varnothing} =\!=$	=	parallel light rays
$\stackrel{\perp}{\Lsh}$	=	central lighting
L^o	=	central light source
$L^o_{1,2,3}$	=	lamp nadir in relation to base of object

Index

Notes and Practice

Notes and Practice

Notes and Practice

Notes and Practice

Notes and Practice

Notes and Practice

Notes and Practice